RUINS TO RUINS

ROLAND WAUER

Copyright © 2022 Roland Wauer.

All rights reserved. No part of this book may be reproduced, stored, or transmitted by any means—whether auditory, graphic, mechanical, or electronic—without written permission of both publisher and author, except in the case of brief excerpts used in critical articles and reviews. Unauthorized reproduction of any part of this work is illegal and is punishable by law.

ISBN: 978-1-957203-95-9 (sc)
ISBN: 978-1-957203-96-6 (hc)
ISBN: 978-1-957203-97-3 (e)

Because of the dynamic nature of the Internet, any web addresses or links contained in this book may have changed since publication and may no longer be valid. The views expressed in this work are solely those of the author and do not necessarily reflect the views of the publisher, and the publisher hereby disclaims any responsibility for them.

One Galleria Blvd., Suite 1900, Metairie, LA 70001
1-888-421-2397

CONTENTS

Acknowledgements..v

Chapter 1   Saba, A Bright Green Gumdrop.................................. 1
Chapter 2   St. Croix 9
Chapter 3   Miami and Uncle Gus 14
Chapter 4   The Yucatan 19
Chapter 5   Cobá, Tulum and Cozumel Island............................... 28
Chapter 6   Cancún to Valladolid... 37
Chapter 7   Chetumal: Kohunlich and Calakmul............................ 45
Chapter 8   Tikal... 53
Chapter 9   Bonampak and Yaxchilan 61
Chapter 10 Palenque 68
Chapter 11 Villahermosa and Catemaco 77
Chapter 12 Oaxaca and Monte Alban 84
Chapter 13 Veracruz: Cerro de Las Mesas and Zemboala.................. 92
Chapter 14 Veracruz: Quiahuiztlan and El Tajín......................... 100
Chapter 15 Zempoala and Popocatépetl................................... 109
Chapter 16 Tula 117
Chapter 17 Mexico City, Texcoco 124
Chapter 18 Mexico City, The National Museum of Anthropology.. 132
Chapter 19 Tenochtitlan 141
Chapter 20 Together 150

ACKNOWLEDGEMENTS

ALTHOUGH THE PEOPLE and their conversations in *Ruins to Ruins* are a figment of my imagination, the ruins and the towns and cities are factual. I have visited all of the ruins included, but the details about the peoples that once inhabited those sites, as well as their behavior, are based upon the historic literature.

I want to thank my friends who shared my various Mexico trips. They include Ben Basham, Betty Gaddis, Dick Russell, Jim and Cilla Tucker, Bo and Woody West, and my wife, Betty Wauer.

Also, I am grateful to Cheryl Johnson for reading my manuscript and providing many helpful suggests. Finally, I thank my editor,??

CHAPTER 1

SABA, A BRIGHT GREEN GUMDROP

ONE MOMENT WE were in flight, staring out of the airplane at the rocky cliff face dangerously close to our right side, then suddenly the wheels touched down and we screeched to a halt. We had arrived on Saba! Never before or since have I experienced such a landing. The runway is located at the very edge of two cliffs to take advantage of the island's one and only flat space – Flat Point. The runway length is just 1,312 feet, and only specially built STOL (short takeoff and landing) DE Haviland Otter aircraft are allowed to land. It is like landing on an aircraft carrier; one little mistake could end it all.

It is amazing that Saba has an airport at all. It is not only a tiny island of only five square miles, less than a speck in the Caribbean Sea, but it also is extraordinary because it rises to a height of 2,845 feet, higher than many of the larger Lesser Antilles. The island sits atop cliffs that drop off into very deep waters; there are no beaches. Saba looks like a giant green pyramid rising out of the deep blue Caribbean Sea. Some of the locals call it the Green Gumdrop.

My flight began on St. Croix in the U.S. Virgin Islands, where I was living. I took a Windward Airline flight to St. Martin and then a twenty-minute flight to Saba. The purpose of my Saba visit was to attend a funeral of a friend that I had met on St. Croix. Martin had worked for the Virgin Islands government for most of his adult life but had retired to Saba following his retirement. His wife was from Saba where her mother still lived. Within a few months of moving to Saba. His wife and her mother had been killed in an automobile accident during a trip to New York City. Within another few months, at the age of 83, Martin had also passed on.

The first thing, after retrieving my bag, was to taxi to Windwardside and Scout's Place, where I had reservations for my three-night stay. Within a few minutes, I had claimed a taxi, or it may be more appropriate to say that Suzane, the friendly taxi driver, had claimed me. I discovered that Suzane was aware of Martin's funeral, and it also seemed that she knew everyone on the island. As we drove away from the airport, I was welcomed by a large a "Welcome to Saba" sign, colorfully decorated with a triggerfish and a hibiscus blossom, an appropriate combination for this tiny island.

As we began our trip up the steep roadway to Windwardside, I could not help but notice the high cliff that served as a backdrop to Cove Bay. And there, sailing along the cliff was a red-billed tropicbird. I asked Suzane to stop along the road, so I could get a better look. Through binoculars I was able to get a superb look at both red-billed and white-tailed tropicbirds. Suzane, who appeared to be known birds, told me that both species nest on the high cliffs during the nesting season. For me, seeing both tropicbirds were a special welcome to this fascinating island.

The winding highway above Flat Point would make anyone admire the ingenuity and skill of its builders. It zigzagged upward through Lower and Upper Hell's Gate (villages) with nineteen curves before topping out at English Quarter and Windwardside. We had climbed 1,899 feet in about five miles. After Suzane delivered me safely at Scout's Place, she remained. I later discovered that she was tending bar at the little restaurant where I ate not long afterwards. I visited with her, over a couple beers, about the island in general, and she offered to drive me to the small cemetery the next day. She also was planning to attend.

"Suzane, you seemed to know Saba extremely well. How long have you lived here?" I asked.

"I have lived here almost all my life. I came here with my folks from Amsterdam when I was a wee girl. Daddy was sent here as an assistant to the governor. And I guess I fell in love with the island, because when my folks returned to Holland, I remained." She continued: "I did go home to visit my parents once, a number of years ago, but I missed my little green island. I hurried back as soon as I could."

She asked how long I intended to stay on the islands, and when I said that I planned on a three-day stay, she asked if I was a hiker. "I plan to hike up Mount Scenery the day after the funeral, and if you are interested, I would welcome your company." She explained that the Mount Scenery hike was something that many of the young people did once each year.

"That is a great idea," I said. "I would love to see more of the island, and the opportunity to climb Mount Scenery is something that I would truly like to do. I hike all over St. Croix when the opportunity arises."

We continued our conversation, and I was so engrossed with her comments about Mount Scenery and various other features on Saba, that I lost track of time. Suddenly she said that she had to close up and go home. She added that the island administrators did not permit any drinking establishment to remain open after the dinner hour. I helped her close up, and before she left for home, we agreed on a time at which she would pick me and drive me to the cemetery. It already was late in the evening, and I climbed into bed soon after reaching my cottage. I fell asleep thinking about hiking with Suzane to the summit of Mount Scenery.

I awoke at dawn, showered and dressed, and wandered toward the restaurant for a bite to eat. The morning was clear and bright. Mount Scenery appeared like a great green haystack dominating the little town of Windwardside. The mountain greenery was more than that of tropical vegetation that morning. The sunlight made it deep velvet green, darker here and there where long drainages, locally called guts, were still filled with nighttime shadows and secrets. The scene was almost magical.

Suzane was, right where I had seen her the night before. "You must spend much of your life here," I said, not able to come up with something cleverer to say.

"Yes, I do," she answered. "I keep busy either working here or driving folks from the airport to their homes or accommodations."

"How do you find time to enjoy other activities, like hiking Mount Scenery?"

"I am able to take off work on occasion, and my sister watches the store, so to speak."

Suzane sat at the little table and visited while I ate a breakfast of coffee and scones. It seemed at first only a fraction what I normally would eat, but the scones, filled with apricot jam, were all that I needed. I asked, "You seem to be a jack-of-all-trades. Did you also make the scones?"

"No," she answered. "Baking is a specialty of my sister, Marianna. She arrives early each morning and prepares the scones and breads." She added; "I don't have that talent, and since I often work late in the restaurant, I sleep later than she does."

The funeral was held in a beautiful glade on the upper side of Windwardside. More than two dozen folks were in attendance, and it appeared that I was the only non-native. The preacher, a Mr. Calvin, seemed to have known Martin for some time, as he extolled his value to the Saba society and proclaimed him to have been a true Christian who had participated in many of the church activities. I, frankly, had not known about that side of my friend during the years that we were neighbors on St. Croix.

I did recall one time seeing him when I attended the Christian church in Fredricksted. But neither of us attended church on a regular basis, although I had heard that he once was an active member. I remembered my mother mentioning him once or twice on seeing him at church.

My mind must have been on other things, such as the hike up Mount Scenery and Suzane, because all of a sudden, I was aware that Mr. Calvin was asking me if I would like to say a few words. Since I was a long-time friend of the deceased and had come to Saba for the single purpose of attending Martin's funeral, I was asked to speak. I quickly stood and walked to the front where I stood near the coffin.

"Thank you, Mr. Calvin," I started. "Martin Genry was a good friend during the years that he lived on St. Croix. Although he was much older, our friendship was mostly due to our mutual interest in nature. We spent one day watching birds at Krouse Lagoon and on another day, we hiked to East End. Martin was a very good naturalist, and he, in a sense, was my mentor in many ways."

It appeared that everyone was paying attention, so I continued, "I recall one adventure when we spent a marvelous day at Salt River Bay. He knew much more than I about that site. I remember being surprised about what he told me that day. Although I had visited the Salt River area several times before, I was unaware that this was where Christopher Columbus landed on his second voyage to the New World, and where ancient Carib

Indians had once lived. Plus, the Spanish, French, English, and Danes had built fortifications at the bay entrance, although little remains." I added, "I was much impressed with his knowledge."

I must also have impressed some of the folks there that day, because afterwards several approached me to say that they were glad that I was able to attend Martin's funeral. One old gentleman thanked me for reminding him about the Salt River site; he had visited the site many years earlier with his parents. He said that they took him there so he could see what they considered the most important historical site in all the Caribbean.

That evening I again ate dinner at the little restaurant where Suzane worked. She joined me as soon as I entered the restaurant, and we shared our meals and conversation again until closing time. I guess I had not truly looked at her earlier, but this evening as we sat close together during the meal, I realized what a beautiful woman she was. Her dark hair and eyes were most striking, and, despite being dressed for work, I could not help but admire her shapely body.

I finally asked her, "Suzane, you appeared to be alone at the funeral, are you not married?"

"Robert," she answered, "I am not married, although when I went to university in Amsterdam, I did become engaged to a fellow student, and we planned to marry after graduation. But I found him with my girlfriend, and I could not continue a serious relationship after that. In fact, I returned to Saba soon afterwards, even before graduation. I guess I am to be alone on my little green island. Perhaps that is one of the reasons that I enjoy talking with someone my own age."

"But Suzane," I said, "You cannot give up hope. You are an amazing woman, and you have so much to offer the right man."

"You know, Robert, there are not any men of my age on Saba, and the only men that have expressed interest are considerably older than I or are already married. And," she added, "I am a 22-year old virgin; I do not know if I could even satisfy a man."

I was unsure how to respond; her honest comment was almost embarrassing, and yet I did not take it as anything but honesty. She was a very appealing woman. However, instead of continuing that conversation, I changed the subject to our hike on Mount Scenery. We were of the same age and I had had several sexual encounters on St. Croix. And yet, I had never had a relationship with anyone such as Suzane.

The following day, I met Suzane at the restaurant, and after breakfast we started our climb up Mount Scenery. And what a climb it was. The trail begins at the edge of Windwardside and immediately is steep and treacherous; it is mostly grown over with vegetation, and we had to step carefully. Actually, the route is less of a hiking trail than a spectacular stairway of 1,046 steps cut into the steep mountain side. It is one of the most remarkable routes in all the West Indies. From the bottom, the 1,046 steps seemed of little consequence. But it soon became apparent that the hike to the top of Saba was going to be more than just walking up a long flight of stairs. The 1,046 steps gain 2,855 feet in less than two miles distance.

It was obvious why stairs were constructed rather than a trail, which would require numerous switchbacks and considerable scarring of the slopes. A trail would have been much longer and costlier, in both construction and maintenance. As it was, the Mount Scenery 'trail' climbed practically straight up the mountainside with only a few diversions. In retrospect, it seemed altogether appropriate for Saba.

The trail began in a gut filled with tropical vegetation, but it soon climbed up to an open ridge, with more stairs that seemed to go directly up the mountain. Most of the plants along the lower half of the route were the same species that grow in and around Windwardside, such as bananas, mangos, soursops, and papayas. The huge mango tree that shaded the start of the trail is one of the largest I have ever seen. It literally dominates the entry area.

Although the vegetation in the lower elevations was locally called tropical forest, the mid-level slopes was considered cloud forest, and near the summit, I found what I thought might be rain forest.

I was impressed with the number of bird songs within each zone. When Suzane expressed interest in the many songs, I was able to point out individual birds or songs that included several Caribbean specialties; Caribbean elaenias, Lesser Antillean bullfinches, and two exquisite hummingbirds, green-throated carib and purple-throated carib. At one point, we stood side-by-side for several minutes as we admired a green-throated carib drinking from a gorgeous red bromeliad.

By the time we reached the summit, we both were exhausted; 1,046 steps have a way of stressing the body. We sat for a long time at the summit, recovering our breath, and admiring the marvelous vistas in all directions. At several places along the trail we had stopped and looked back down into the streets of Windwardside to see how it hugs the little ridge above the sea. Suzane pointed out her house and also the school she had attended. The scene from our vantage point, with the abundance of red-roofed buildings, surrounded by colorful vegetation, was truly impressive.

After several minutes, I took our lunches out of the backpack that I had been carrying, and we sat there side-by-side eating her very tasty sandwiches and admiring our surroundings. Her very nearness was almost overpowering.

It was Suzane who first asked a personal question; she was curious about any close relationships I might have on St. Croix. I told her that I have had a couple girlfriends but none that I would build a life with.

"I am still very young and have much of my life ahead of me. I want to travel and see the world before settling down."

Things began to happen in a hurry. I don't remember now how the first kiss began, but we suddenly were kissing, and very soon we were lying back on the grass and holding each other extremely tightly and continuing to kiss. Soon the kissing increased to the point where I had a difficult time controlling myself. We were making love while still completely dressed. I found myself touching her lovely breasts and squeezing her more tightly. "Suzane," I said, "I want more, but I will stop if you want me to." And immediately she responded: "Oh, Robert, I want more, too."

We helped each other undress, and we continued our love-making without the hindrance of clothes. That first time with Suzane, near the summit of Mount Scenery, was one of the most exciting and intense sex I had ever experienced. Afterwards we lay side-by-side for several minutes while she expressed her wonderment about that new experience. And in another few minutes, she straddled me, and our kissing was even more passionate. Very soon, we made love a second time.

We had become so involved with one another that we had not noticed that we were engulfed with clouds. What could we have expected in a cloud forest at mid-day? We immediately dressed and began out trek back down the mountainside. And we were forced to move extremely slowly;

the steps were even slicker than they were on our ascent. And by the time we reached Windwardside, we were both thoroughly soaked. And yet we clutched each other for several minutes before she left me at my cottage door and went on to her nearby home.

Suzane had taken the entire day off from work so she was not at the restaurant when I got there after a hot shower and a change into dry clothes. I had taken time to fully recover from our descent from Mount Scenery. Her sister, Marianne, was there, and when I asked her about Suzane she told me that she was not well and was staying home.

My major concern that evening was that I was scheduled to fly back to St. Croix early the next day, and I wanted to talk to Suzane first. I asked Marianne, "Can you contact Suzane and ask her to meet me?"

Without even looking at me, she answered, "She told me about what happened on your hike, and she is too embarrassed to see you."

"But," I said, "I care for Suzane a great deal, and I want to see her. Is there not some way that you could arrange that?"

Her answer was "No, I know that she does not want to see you. She wants to forget the entire affair."

With that, I was truly surprised. She had told me that there was no one on the island she could marry. I thought that we had found a good relationship and I had hoped to continue seeing her. I asked, "But why would she not want to see me?"

Marianne's answer totally surprised me. "Robert, Suzane is soon to be married to a fine man that our parents approve of, and any additional contact with you would very likely jeopardize that opportunity. Please, leave it alone."

What more could I say? I had totally misjudged the situation, and I was soon to leave Saba. Perhaps it was best to leave well enough alone and move on.

CHAPTER 2

ST. CROIX

I WAS UNSETTLED on my flight home to St. Croix. I felt that my departure from Saba was like being cast aside. But I consoled myself, realizing that the entire relationship with Suzane had occurred over only a three-day period. Yet, even then I had begun to care, more than I would have expected. And to learn that she was soon to be married, after our short affair, bothered me immensely. I wondered if I had been used, and yet she appeared to be an honest and good person. But that experience was now in the past, and it was time to get on with my life.

The trip to Saba to attend the funeral of my friend had occurred after I had finished my final year at the University of the Virgin Islands, and it was now time to find a job and settle down. My parents welcomed me home and asked about my trip. I told them only about the funeral and my hike up Mount Scenery. My father seemed especially interested in Saba's environment.

"Robert," he said, "tell me about the different habitats you found on Mount Scenery." My father taught agronomy at the university, so it was only natural that he was curious about Saba's natural environment. He added, "I once was offered a job on Saba, but it was in a very different field from my interest. Plus," he added, "your mother was not ready to leave St. Croix; she considers St. Croix her very own 'little green island,' as you have heard her say many times."

I did my best to describe the various habitats on Saba, especially the vegetative zones I had encountered during my climb up Mount Scenery. He asked several questions that I was able to answer reasonably well. After all, since I was a tiny tot, my father had taught me all that I knew about nature. He was most attentive, and following the rather extensive question and answer period, he said, "Robert, I am very proud of you for your knowledge of the natural world. You should consider teaching; you would make a superb teacher."

"Thank you for your confidence in me, but I first want to see more of the natural world that surrounds us for myself."

Abruptly he changed the topic. "Robert, your mother and I have been talking about your future now that you have finished your education on St. Croix, and we know you would do very well with additional education. With that in mind, we have contacted Aunt Helene and Uncle Gus in Florida about the possibility of you living with them and going to a university nearby. They have agreed if you are interested."

I was surprised at what was said, as I had not given any serious thought of leaving St. Croix. And yet I had no idea about what possible job I might find here on the island. My father continued, "You know that we cannot afford to send you to a university unless you could live with someone who would provide room and board."

"Sir," I responded, "that would be marvelous, but I would have a difficult time leaving St. Croix. Here is where home is and my many friends. I cannot even remember Aunt Helene and Uncle Gus; are you sure they would be willing to put me up?" I recalled the one time they had visited us on St. Croix, and I remember that Aunt Helene was very nice and sweet, but I had the opposite feeling about Uncle Gus. He was very argumentative during the few days they were visiting, and I also thought that he was more interested in visiting the Cruzan rum factories than seeing the various sites that they were taken to around the island.

My father said, "Robert, please consider our suggestion. Schools in Florida will not start up for another two months, but you would need to register within the next two or three weeks. And that can be done through a local office in St. Thomas."

My mother, who was also present in the room, had not said a word during our conversation. Finally, she turned to me and said, "Robert, as much as we would miss you if you went away to college, we think that this opportunity should not be ignored. You are too smart to end up in the cane fields or working at one of the rum factories. If you are to make something of yourself, you must acquire a higher education that would allow you to become whatever you want to be."

Looking at my mother, I could see how serious she was; she had a difficult time hiding the tears in her eyes. Although my father was rather stoic, I could tell that they had thoroughly discussed the idea of me leaving the island for further education on the mainland. I was unsure what to say, so I simply said, "Thank you so much for making contact with Aunt Helene and Uncle Gus about me living with them, and especially thank you for the concern you have for my future." I added, "Please let me think about this a few days and I will make a decision very soon." With that it appeared that the subject was shelved for the time being.

But I also asked, "Sir, I am unsure why you are suggesting that I attend college in Florida?"

He responded, "We have considered that, but we also know that if you are going to make anything special of yourself in the field of biology you will need an advanced education off-island. On-island education leads only to working within the rum industry. I know that you could find a job in one of the rum factories, and probably would work your way up to a high-level management position, but you deserve more. You need to see more of the world. You are a naturalist at heart. You should travel and learn more than what is possible on the islands."

I thanked my parents for their compliments and once again stated that I would give all that they had suggested my full consideration.

I was anxious to talk with my best friend, Johnny, about this opportunity. Although Johnny was older than I and had attended a college in Florida, I thought he might be helpful to me in a decision about what to do.

So, the next day I rode over to the Martins' house to talk with Johnny. I found him working in the yard, tending to the large garden that his parents had established. It was beautiful plot with dozens of flowering plants. And before we began our conversation, we stood there and admired the hummingbirds that were feeding there. Nowhere else on St. Croix could one find the number of hummingbirds that used the Martins' garden. Both green-throated caribs and Antillean crested hummingbirds were there, zipping here and there in their efforts to check every one of the flowering plants. I estimated that, during my stay at the garden, as many as eight or ten individuals were feeding at any time. And right alongside the hummers were two or three bananaquits, locally known as sugarbirds.

"Johnny," I said, "I need your advice about an opportunity my folks mentioned yesterday. They suggested that I go to Florida and attend college. They even went so far as to contact my aunt and uncle who live there for a place where I could live."

"You're kidding me," he answered. "That would be a wonderful opportunity for you. What are you concerned about? Man, I would jump at such an opportunity if it were me."

"I have two concerns, I guess. One is I am not sure what my major might be, and second, I am concerned about living with my aunt and uncle. She is a very nice person, but he can be a real ass."

"Although I can not address your living situation, I know what you would study. You are already an amazing naturalist; why would you not study biology?"

I thought about that for a few minutes and said, "You are right about a major. My love for nature, especially birds, would fit perfectly. But I would be required to take numerous other subjects that I, frankly, would not care about."

"But think about how quickly you learned about the plant life of St. Croix, and how you were able to identify life zones wherever you are. I am sure that you would find botany especially interesting." Johnny stopped briefly and added some advice: "Do you remember me telling you about that test that I took when I was going to college, when I knew the question perfectly, but I did not answer the question as was intended. So, I got a poor grade. The secret is to listen carefully and to make notes of what is said so you can answer questions that directly responds to the specific questions on the test."

I talked with Johnny for a good hour or more, and he gave me good advice about what might lie in store for me if I decide to go to college in Florida.

Before going to sleep that night, I lay in bed for two long hours thinking about what possibilities were available to me. By morning, I had not reached a decision. I spent the day working around the house, helping my mother with various tasks.

The next day, I took the shuttle boat over to St. Thomas to talk with the folks that operated the small office that had been set up to help Virgin Islanders interested in colleges in Florida. A Mr. Bertran was at once a great help.

"Robert," he told me, "if you plan to live in the North Miami area, you should consider Miami Dade College. It offers a wide range of majors and they are very interested in helping young men from the Caribbean islands. I have talked to those folks about Cruzans such as you, and I am sure they would be most helpful. What would you plan to study; what major might you prefer?"

"Sir," I said, "I am most interested in biology, courses that might lead to work in the field of ornithology or comparable areas."

"Robert, you could not go wrong then, as Miami Dade offers several courses in biology, and those could very well lead into the field that you would prefer."

Our conversation lasted for more than an hour, and by the time I left his office and caught the shuttle back to St. Croix, I had pretty well decided that Miami Dade was my best bet. It was very close to where my aunt and uncle lived, even so close that I might be able to walk. It seemed like a natural.

By the time I visited with my parents about what I had learned, I was starting to get excited about the possibilities that lay ahead.

CHAPTER 3

MIAMI AND UNCLE GUS

THE PAN-AM FLIGHT from St. Croix to Miami went without a hitch. And Aunt Helene was waiting for me at the baggage claim. She seemed truly pleased to see me; it had been several years since she and Uncle Gus had visited us on St. Croix, and I was a bit uncertain on seeing her, but she did her best to welcome me and make me feel comfortable. She first asked about my flight, and then she asked about my parents; she was my father's sister and had grown up on St. Croix. She met Uncle Gus there when he was working on a construction job. They had fallen in love and moved to Florida after Gus's job in St. Croix job had finished.

"My parents ask me to give you their love, and they mentioned how long it has been since you and Uncle Gus came to St. Croix. They both told me to tell you that they hope that we can all get back together soon. My parents have been saving for my educations and they are happy that I can stay with you folks during my schooling. I am afraid that a trip to Miami for them is out of the question at this time."

I was amazed at Miami. It was a huge, huge city, so much larger than my little town of Fredricksted on St. Croix where I had lived all my life. In fact, except for one trip to San Juan, Puerto Rico to receive medical care for my father, I had never before been away from the islands of St. Croix and St. Thomas. I found Miami to be so large that I was doubtful if I could actually live in such a place even just to attend college. Almost immediately I began to doubt the logic of leaving St. Croix.

Aunt Helene and Uncle Gus lived in a very nice house on the northern edge of Miami. It contained a large front room, a mid-sized kitchen with a dinning area, three bedrooms, two bathrooms, one of which was connected to what was to be my room, and a large backyard where they had a mid-sized garden. Aunt Helene was proud of her garden and said that she would like to show it to me in the morning. Uncle Gus was not at home when we arrived. Aunt Helene explained that Uncle Gus often stopped for a drink with his friends after work. And she also told me that by the time he came home, oftentimes after midnight, he went straight to bed. There seemed to be little relationship between him and Aunt Helene.

I had grown up in a home with loving parents and two brothers who got along well most of the time. The five of us were what most folks thought of as a close Christian family. I, perhaps, was the one member of the family that did not always conform. My mother explained that "Robert is too much of an adventurer and nature-lover to fit in all the time." That is not to say that I was not loved and nurtured as much as my siblings. In fact, the family often commented that "Robert was the favorite" because he and father were so much alike and constantly together in the outdoors. And that was true; I cherished my time with my father. That was when he taught me about our natural surroundings. He seemed to know a lot about any subject that I asked about. He was especially knowledgeable about the birds, those that were fulltime residents as well as those that only passed through the islands in migration and those that were resident only in winter. I was truly blessed to have such a mentor as my father.

Uncle Gus did not put in his appearance until long after dinner. And when he did, he ignored both Aunt Helene and me and went directly to his room and slammed the door. Aunt Helene explain his behavior as being worn out from his construction job and let it go with that.

The next morning, Aunt Helene and I ate breakfast together; Uncle Gus had already left for work. Soon after breakfast we took a long walk, perhaps as much as three or four miles. That was when she showed me the area of Miami where I was to live, and we also walked by Miami Dade College where I was to start classes in few days. We walked inside, and I talked to a lady in the admissions office; I introduced myself and received a packet of reading material that is handed out to all freshmen. I must admit that I was impressed with the college and grounds. And by the time we wandered around campus a little, I was looking forward to this next stage in my life.

But that next stage was not to be! When Uncle Gus got home that evening he was in a rage. He and Aunt Helene began a loud verbal argument about my presence; Uncle Gus shouted that they "could not afford to keep and feed a damn foreigner." The longer the argument continued, despite Aunt Helene's attempt to keep it under control, the worse it became. She did get Gus into another room, but his ravings were so loud and vehement that I am sure that the next-door neighbors heard it all. And suddenly their door burst open and Gus stormed out, heading for the front door. In passing, he yelled at me that I had better not be there when he came home from work the next day. I, honestly, was frightened; Gus was huge, and it was very obvious that he was drunk.

I hardly slept at all that night. I could not get the image of his shouting and his angry comments out of my head. By morning, however, things seemed to have calmed down. Aunt Helene fixed breakfast and tried to sound like everything would be OK; Gus would get over his opposition and I was "not to worry." Although she tried to hide her appearance, I could see that she had a huge bruise on the left side of her face and her eye was partly closed. I knew then that I would not be able to stay there. She tried to apologize to me by explaining that "Gus gets that way only when drinking," but she also admitted that he drank almost every day after work.

She told me that she planned on talking to a friend down the street a few houses to see if I could possibly stay there. She said that their daughter had recently gone away to college in Virginia, and they had a room not in use at the moment. She apologized again and again for last night's incident, but I knew for sure that I would not remain with my aunt and uncle.

That was when I remembered that I had met a young man, a little older than I, on my flight to Miami. He had given me his name and address in Miami, and he had told me to look him up if time allowed. He had been traveling around the Caribbean exploring many of the islands and their birdlife. He said that he had been studying archeology but was also interested in birds. I told him, "I too am interested in birds; maybe we could get together in Miami and check out some of Miami's better birding areas."

"I would like that very much, but I will be leaving for Mexico very soon," he said. He was planning a trip to Mexico to visit a number of archeological sites. And when I told him that I too would love to see some of Mexico and its fabulous birdlife, he had invited me to go with him.

I decided that I would contact my friend and ask about his upcoming Mexico trip and the possibility of going with him. It took me a good part the day to find his street, after asking directions several times and to walk the four or more miles to his house. Before leaving the house, I told Aunt Helene that I had already made arrangements to leave Miami for Mexico. I didn't attempt to further explain myself; I think she was thankful that I had somewhere else to go and would not be there when Uncle Gus got home.

My friend from the plane, Johnathan Cruz, was totally surprised when he came to his door to find me with my suitcase and backpack standing there. He immediately invited me inside where we sat and I explained my predicament. He was very gracious and welcoming. When I told him that I would love to join him on his Mexico adventure, he was excited.

"Robert," he said, "you do not know how glad I am that you appeared out of the blue. My companion who was going with me told me just yesterday that he had to back out because his mother is ill. They are taking her to New York for treatment, and he will be going with her. They think that her treatment will be extensive, and he is obligated to remain with her." He added, "I already have purchased tickets, and you are welcome to use one of them."

"Also, you are welcome to stay here until our trip, and I want you to meet my father. I told him about you and how we seemed to be compatible. He is a local banker, and he should be home by mid-afternoon." He added that his mother had passed away two years ago. "But," he said, "We have a housekeeper, Margaret, who takes care of the house and cooks our meals. And by the way, she is from St. Lucia, and she is a marvelous cook. You will love her meals."

I thanked him profusely for his hospitality and I said "I am curious why you are so interested in Mexico; there are lots of other places to visit that have birds you probably have not seen."

His answer surprised me: "Mexico has more than birds. I also have a keen interest in archeology, and Mexico has some amazing restored ruins, and many more have been uncovered only recently. I have read everything available about those sites, but I want to see them for myself. Plus," he added, "Many of those sites are located in areas with amazing birdlife."

"Johnathan," I said, "I have little knowledge about Mexico's archeology. I have heard about a couple sites, Uxmal and Chichén Itza, and the idea of visiting those sites with someone like you who has knowledge of those early civilizations would be wonderful."

I could not believe my luck. That morning I had been so down that I was thinking about going back to St. Croix, and now I had a place to stay, meals, and a friend. And even more, it also seemed that I was about to go off on an adventure to Mexico. And even his father seemed genuinely pleased with me and that Johnathan had company for his Mexico adventure.

That evening, before going to bed, I wrote a long and honest letter to my parents, explaining what happened at the Martin house and my move to a friend's home. I felt guilty about telling them about the Martin situation, but I felt that they should know the truth. I also felt guilty about not attending college as expected. I felt even guiltier when I told them that I was going to use some of the money they gave me for college for a trip to Mexico.

"Please understand these changes," I wrote. "I will write again very soon to tell you about Mexico and the many new birds I hope to see. Your loving son, Robert."

CHAPTER 4

THE YUCATAN

OUR AERO MEXICO flight to Mérida, the capitol of Yucatan, arrived in record time, and we soon took a taxi to the Hacienda Inn, where we had reservations. We had also reserved a car for the next several days. By the time we secured our room and vehicle, it was too late to wander around town, so we had a late dinner in the hotel's restaurant and settled in for the night. I had discovered that Johnathan spoke fluent Spanish, while I could barely manage. I did know enough words to order a meal and ask directions, but I was never sure what I had ordered or where I was going.

During dinner, we discussed our plans for the next few days. "I want to see as many of the Mayan ruins as possible," he said. "I am particularly interested in Chichén Itza and Uxmal, but there are dozens of others scattered all over the Yucatan. I also want to visit the Aztec site of Tenochtitlan, if possible."

"I, too, am interested in seeing the ruins, but I also want to see as many Mexican birds as possible. I am especially interested in species that are Mexican endemics."

Johnathan already had a guide book that included maps of the Yucatan, so soon after breakfast we were en route to Chichén Itza, about 75 miles from Mérida. I could tell that Johnathan was excited about seeing what many people regard as the finest Mayan ruins.

He told me a little about the site as we drove. "The name is a Mayan term that means "Mouth of the Well of the Itza," and *itza* means water wizards. Although Chichén has been known for many years, the site is now being reconstructed based upon recent findings and updated analysis. One thing is sure, it is one of the largest and best restored of approximately fifty-thousand registered Mayan sites on the Yucatan Peninsula."

"Wow, I had no idea there were so many sites within the Yucatan. Are there others that have been restored?"

"A few others have, but Chichén and Uxmal are the two best, at least of those already known. Archeologists tell us that the Chichén area has been occupied continuously since at least 1000 B.C. The earliest Maya-speaking inhabitants were farmers, who lived in straw or wooden huts and grew corn. But, beginning about 250 A.D., there was a major cultural change that flourished until the late 600s. During that period, the Mayan priests gained greater power, because of a perceived necessity for ceremonies and human sacrifices to ensure the production of crops. And for whatever reason, this period was followed by a time of quiescence."

I could hardly believe what he was telling me, but I knew that Johnathan was a scholar, and I realized that much of his earlier studies had involved Mayan history.

"Johnathan, I had no idea you were so interested in the Mayan; no wonder you are so excited about this trip. Where did you learn so much about the Mayans? Does the Miami library have a good number of books about Mayan history?"

"Yes and no. I did find a few history books in the library, but none that I did not have available at home. Something you didn't know, but my father studied archeology when he was at the university in Miami. He acquired many books on archeology, and I think he became obsessed with the Mayan civilization." He added, "It was not the Mayans that welcomed Cortez when he landed in 1852 near what is now Veracruz. It was the Aztecs. If we are able, I would love to visit a few Aztec sites as well."

I did not answer him, although I was amazed at how much he seemed to known about early Mexico history. He turned to me, expecting my response, but we had arrived at entrance to Chichén and I was looking into the top of a huge tree at the edge of the compound. "What are you watching?" he asked.

"Look in that tree; there must be two dozen birds feeding on what I guess is fruit in that one tree." And immediately we both were studying the abundant birds. I counted at least 60 black and yellow or gold orioles of five different kinds: Altimira, orange, orchard, hooded, and yellow-backed orioles. They all were feeding on the tree's small and inconspicuous green-brown flowers. Individuals and groups of three or four orioles came and went during the next 30 or 40 minutes while we watched the flowering kapok tree. We also identified at least four kinds of hummingbirds there. Cinnamon hummingbirds were most common, but a wedge-tailed saberwing, green-breasted mango, and buff-bellied hummingbird were feeding at the flowers, too.

"You know, with what we are watching at the moment, I could almost forget the ruins" he said. In another several minutes, he added, "There are a number of other birds feeding there. Wow, that tree is alive with birds." I began ticking off the species I was seeing. "I see golden-olive and red-vented woodpeckers, tropical kingbird, social and boat-billed fycatchers, blue-gray gnatcatcher, clay-colored robin, rufus-browed peppershrike, four species of warblers – Tennessee, black-and-white, yellow-throated, and black-throated green – and several yellow-winged tanagers. It's like an avian smorgasbord!"

The flowering tree was a kapok, a species we both were familiar with. But what made those bird sightings so extra special was that it occurred within the beautiful grounds of Hacienda Chichén at Chichén Itza. What made our observations extra special was that the branches of the trees were mostly bare, providing us a great opportunity to see the birds in the open. There were several other trees nearby, but none of the others possessed such sweet flowers as our very own kapok.

After paying a small entrance fee and purchasing a guidebook, we were wandering the grounds of Chichén Itza. Birds were everywhere we looked. It took us several more minutes, and several more avian sightings, before we began to pay attention to the ruins.

The physical remains of Chichén Itza are scattered throughout a three-square-mile-area that contains hundreds of restored buildings and ruins. The largest and most imposing structure is El Castillo, the castle. It is a four-sided 78-foot high pyramid that was constructed for the worship of Kukulcan. The structure has a flight of 91 steps on each side. Ninety-one times four equals 364; these, plus the upper platform represent the 365 days of the year. Inside this structure is an earlier temple that contains a red painted chac mool (a jaguar-like figurine) set with seventy-three pieces of jade.

The ninety steps to the top platform were enticing, and we soon were climbing. But our ascent was not as easy as we imagined. Each step was deep, so instead of running up several steps at a time, we had to take one at a time, but the view from the top made it all worthwhile. We both sat for a considerable time, admiring the scene around us.

"Amazing! From this viewpoint, you can see most of the Yucatan Peninsula. You can see how flat the entire area is."

"Indeed. This is a marvelous view," Johnathan said. A few minutes later, he added: "Let's go take a look at that round tower."

We climbed back down the stairs and walked over to what was called the "Caracol Observatory." This was a 48-foot-high circular tower built upon three great platforms. The tower contains a circular interior staircase that has given it the name *carcol*, meaning snail in Spanish. The tower has slits and holes in the upper part, which were used to align the stars, sun, and moon for study. The Mayans were able to calculate the cyclic motion of the earth, and their calendar was more exact than any other the world has known. Two hundred years before the birth of Christ, they developed a calendar that lost only two hours every 381 years. The modern Gregorian calendar loses 24 hours every four years. The Mayans were the first people to understand the abstract concept of zero and computed a figure of 365.2420 days for every year. Our modern time measuring techniques tell us that the solar year spans 365.2411 days.

Most of this information was included within the guidebook we had purchased, and Johnathan was reading aloud as we wandered through the compound. On one occasion, while we were sitting on a bench under a huge red-flowering tree, two young ladies suddenly appeared, and we found ourselves talking with them. They were German students, but they spoke very good English. I wondered later if they had attached themselves to us for the opportunity to speak English with someone who spoke native English.

Johnathan, however, disagreed. He told me "No, the reason they were attracted to us was simply our magnetic personalities."

In truth, I didn't care what the reason might have been, because we ended up as a group of four all during remainder of our stay at Chichén Itza. When we drove back to Mérida later in the day, they followed us, and we all ate supper together.

The next stop that first day at Chichén was the great ballcourt. It is said to be the largest and finest in all Mesoamerica, and it had been restored to the point that one could easily imagine the fierce games that were played there. Losers were sacrificed! Relief panels at the base of the walls depict losers being prepared for their death. The court consists of two parallel walls 272 feet long and separated by a playing field 199 feet wide. A stone ring, depicting a serpent, is situated twenty-three feet above the ground at each end. The purpose of the game was to control a hard rubber ball, using only the athlete's elbows, hips and knees, and to pass the ball through the ring. The game was part of a religious rite, and the ball was symbolic of the sun; it was not permitted to touch the ground.

Gretchen, the young lady that seemed to stay at my side most of the time, was anxious to see the sacred well. So, we wandered over to that side of the compound to take a look. It is situated at the end of the 300-yard "sacred causeway," which begins at the end of the Platform of Venus, a ceremonial-dance platform. The well, locally known as a *cenote*, is a natural sinkhole two-hundred feet across and filled with water to approximately sixty-five feet below the rim. The water has been measured at forty feet deep and there are another ten feet of mud below that.

While looking into the cenote, Johnathan said, "Archeological studies suggest that Chichén's cenote was used to sacrifice humans as well as valuable objects to the rain god, Chac, especially during period of drought. Underwater explorations have discovered fifty human skeletons, many precious stones, and another four thousand pieces of odds and ends of everyday Mayan life. The bottom of the well provided archeologists with a rich midden of materials that helped them piece together much of the Chichén Itza puzzle."

We were impressed with Johnathan's knowledge of Chichén, and the three us told him so. He seemed surprisingly embarrassed with our praise. I had not seen that about him before. Later I chided him, saying that Marian, the girl that he was closest to, was the one who had been most responsible for praising him. His response was an odd-sounding "ya."

Our guidebook included details about water on the Yucatán. Water has always been a scarce commodity, and the sacred well was undoubtedly the reason that Chichén Itza was situated here. Almost all the Yucatán Peninsula is made of limestone. Rainfall runs off immediately, seeping into underground channels and lakes. Before pumps came into being, water was available only where caves occurred or where the surface layers had caved in to form natural sinkholes. Chichén's sacred cenote was one example.

We also were impressed with the forest surrounding the Chichén compound. Tall vegetation abuts the compound, and our guidebook included a description of several tree species. One of those is known as the "fish poison tree," or *habib*. It is a small tree that develops long, thick, flanged seedpods. When the toxic seeds are thrown into streams, they poison the fish, and the Mayans used that method of fishing. Gretchen was attracted to a small tree that the guidebook called *chacab*, but I recognized it as gumbo limbo, a species that occurs on St. Croix as well as in Florida. It is notable for its peeling reddish bark.

All and all, by the time we left Chichén and returned to Mérida, we had had a fascinating day. I had completely enjoyed the ruins and my companions. The four of us had dinner together that evening and by the time we parted for our own rooms we had decided to spend the next day together for a visit to Uxmal.

In the morning, after breakfast and packing up, we drove south about forty miles, planning to stay overnight at the Hotel Hacienda Uxmal. We were fortunate to obtain two rooms at Uxmal, even though we did not have reservations.

En route to Uxmal, we had one exciting event. We had found a pull-off and a trail at kilometer post 16, where we ate a quick lunch that we had bought at Mérida, and we walked into the forest. Almost immediately we saw an ornate hawk-eagle that was perched in a huge bread-nut tree. It seemed to think it was well hidden and sat there until we all had an excellent look at this beautiful raptor. A pair of masked tityras and a white-lored gnatcatcher were found in the same tree. We could hear blue ground-doves calling nearby; they were surprisingly abundant within those woods. We also added dusky antbird, rufous piha, sulphur-rumped flycatcher, long-billed gnatwren, and red-crowned ant-tanager to our growing Yucatán bird list.

Although the women did not have their own binoculars, Johnathan and I shared our binoculars each time we found an especially attractive bird. Gretchen was truly excited about seeing birds 'up-close.' She said, "I have never before watched birds, and you are making a bird-watcher of me."

During the remainder of the time we spent together watching birds, she continued to be excited by each observation.

Although neither Johnathan or I had claimed either girl, they chose for themselves. I was especially glad that Gretchen had attached herself to me. Right from the start I could imagine us sharing a bed, but none of us seemed to have enough courage to suggest such a thing.

The Uxmal ruins represent the best preserved of all the pure Mayan cities in Mexico. The guidebook stated that the Uxmal region did not, unlike that at Chichén, reflect the Mexican culture. This city had been constructed between 500 and 1000 A.D. and was abandoned at the height of its development. Unlike most other Yucatán settlements, which were built around a cenote, Uxmal citizens used cisterns to collect rainwater; some of them are still in use.

"But why did they desert such an extensive city?" Gretchen asked.

Johnathan answered, "Archeologists are unsure, but many of them believe that the entire Yucatan suffered a severe drought, and most of the inhabitants were forced to move elsewhere."

Of all the Uxmal ruins, I was most impressed with the Pyramid of the Magicians. It stands 125 feet high and is oval rather than rectangle. It really is five different temples in one; five openings along the face of the pyramid lead to one of the five temples.

Johnathan said that, more than any of the other ruins, he had especially looked forward to seeing the Pyramid of the Magicians. Again acting as our tour guide, he said, "The Pyramid of the Magicians was built over a three-hundred-year period. The base is Temple One, the oldest, and was dated at 569 A.D. It is ornately decorated with masks of the rain god Chac. Temple Two has a pillared inner chamber that was constructed high above ground level and can be reached by a staircase. Temple Three was built onto the rear of Temple Two but was later covered over."

At this point, Marian said, "Why would they destroy Temple Two and build another temple over Temple Two?" Johnathan did not have a good answer but said, "I suppose, like most bureaucratic organizations, a new priest probably wanted to establish his own temple."

He continued his comments about the structure: "Temple Four sits on top of the oval base and can be entered through the jaws of a stylized mask. And Temple Five is a rectangular structure at the very top of the pyramid. It can be reached by 150 steps that are flanked by masks which depict the rain god."

We spend much of the day wandering around the compound, and I was surprised to see that it was considerable smaller than that of Chichén Itza. I learned that the entire city, which consists of 15 to 20 ruins, were all within the relatively small area of less than half a square mile. As we wandered about, we also watched for species of birds we had not already seen.

Suddenly, Marian pointed at a bird that was flying across the compound and said, "Look at that bird with a red head! What is that?"

We immediately looked to where she was pointing. The bird had flown to a post and was sitting still. "That my friends is a royal flycatcher, another of the Mexican specialties," I answered. "It shows its bright red crest during the breeding season. The rest of the year its crest is held flat on its head, giving it a hammerhead profile. Thank you, Marian, that is one great bird!"

Once back in Mérida, we again ate dinner at the hotel restaurant and spent a couple hours walking around town. The downtown plaza with filled with young people, sitting together or walking about holding hands. Gretchen grabbed my hand, and we walked side-by-side.

Eventually she said, "Robert, you know we leave in the morning, and I will miss you. You and Johnathan have been so wonderful to us. I would like you to share my bed tonight. I think you would like that, too. But please do not think we German women are promiscuous. We just are not too timid to seek what we want. If you are interested, I would like to share your bed tonight."

We drove the women to the airport the next morning, and I must admit that afterwards I missed their cheery countenance. We agreed that it was too bad that they were scheduled to head home to Germany. They had been an enjoyable addition to our tour of the Yucatan. And the sex the night before had been a special bonus.

But we had more ruins to see. When we discussed our travel plans with the man at the car rental office, he had recommended that we should visit two additional sites, Mayapan and Cobá. "Mayapan," he said, "is nearby and Cobá is further away, but everyone I have recommended these sites to have thanked me when they returned their cars."

Although we already had planned to see Cobá, we had not included Mayapan in our plans. After talking it over, we decided to continue with our plan to see Cobá first and Mayapan later, after our return to Mérida.

CHAPTER 5

COBÁ, TULUM AND COZUMEL ISLAND

OUR ROUTE THAT day took us west almost completely across the Yucatan, about 140 miles. On arriving at Cobá, it was obvious that the site was still in the process of opening to tourism, and we obtained accommodations at the brand-new Villas Arqueologicas, a hotel operated by Club Meditterané, a French corporation. Our dinner that evening was superb! After dinner, I told Johnathan, "This may be our best meal on our entire trip. And our room is so new it still smells new."

Cobá is a Mayan word meaning "wind-ruffled water" and is one of Mexico's largest and most unusual archeological sites. It covers 20 square miles within the heart of Yucatan's rain forest. It forms the hub of a system of ceremonial roads called *sacbeob*, Mayan for "white roads," that radiated out to 16 other Mayan cities. The "white roads" term was used because the Mayans had built them over stone-and-rubble and coated them with white limestone.

The central area of Cobá includes more than 6,000 structures, but only a few have been excavated and studied. The largest of these, El Castillo, stands 138 feet tall and measures 180 by 200 feet at the base; it is the largest Indian structure on the entire Yucatan. One hundred and twenty steps lead up through six terraces to the highest platform, from which the view was spectacular. Although the climb to the top was tiring, the view provided us with a perspective unique for the Yucatan; the entire area is dotted with small freshwater lakes. The numerous structures poking above the dense and bright-green forest, combined with the sparkling blue dots of water, gave the area a colorful and mystical character.

I could not help but express my surprise at the abundance of fresh water. "Johnathan," I asked, "were you aware that this part of the Yucatan, unlike everywhere else we have seen, is so wet?"

"I had no idea, although I do remember my father once mentioning that this part of the Yucatan had very different vegetation than elsewhere. I wondered at the time about what unique wildlife might be found there. And now, here we are, about to see for ourselves."

As we wandered the grounds, we examined a number of stelae, stone pedestals covered with hieroglyphs. While we examined one of the stelae, a uniformed guard approached us and began to tell us about the stelae and the ruins. He introduced himself as Eduardo and said that he had worked there for many years, first as an amateur archeologist and, after the area was opened to tourists, he was hired as an interpreter because he spoke very good English. We found Eduardo to be a very friendly gentleman and a fount of knowledge.

"To date," he said, "thirty-two stelae have been uncovered among the ruins. We believe they were designed to commemorate special events in the Mayan lives, and often included specific dates of events. They have been dated from 634 to 800 A.D., but Cobá remained active well into the middle of the fifteenth century."

Continuing, Eduardo said, "The story of Cobá's human history is still very little known, and excavations and research are actively underway. It will be many years before we know all there is to know about this site."

The surrounding rain forest seemed pristine and even the second growth forest was little disturbed. With Eduardo as our guide, we entered the forest, where he told us about the diversity of trees. The most obvious species, we were told, were the chicle and bread-nut trees. The latter species had six-inch-long evergreen leaves that felt leathery to the touch. Their gray to reddish trunks often forms large buttresses at their base. And the plum-like fruit are edible, tasting a little like spicy potatoes. Eduardo said, "They can be eaten raw, but more importantly can be ground into meal and used for making bread and tortillas." He also pointed out mahogany, gumbo limbo, papelillo, kapok, cigarbox, and chicle trees. Johnathan said that he wished that his botanist father could see the abundant trees within the Cobá landscape.

"Tell us about the chicle trees," I said.

"Yes, indeed. The native chicle tree, called *ya* or *palo maria*, is one of the area's most important plants. It furnishes very durable wood, and its fruit, locally known as *sapodilla*, is considered one of the very best in Latin America. The latex, when mixed with sugar, glucose syrup and a flavoring, produces chewing gum."

"Can you tell us about the full process?" I asked.

"Indeed. The latex-gathering process is rather complex. The tall grayish trunks are first cleared of loose bark to about thirty feet high. Slanted incisions are cut in a herringbone pattern, and the tree is allowed to drain for twenty-four hours. The thick, gooey substance seeps downward from one cut to the next and collects in a leather pouch attached below the lowest cut. That material is boiled with water and any impurities are removed. It is then poured into wooden molds lined with leaves and left to harden. The hard blocks can be stored or transported to market."

"Can each tree sustain constant bleeding?"

"No, each tree can be tapped only three times before it must be left for four years to allow it to recover enough to be tapped again."

Eduardo stayed with us for a considerable time, but he left us soon after we began spending more time looking at birds than looking at the trees.

We recorded 94 species of birds during our two-day exploration of Cobá. The numerous lakes provided a habitat that is unusual in the Yucatan, and we added several species that preferred that habitat. Most surprising of these was a pair of black skimmers that cruised back and forth over Laguna de Cobá all day, seeming to be out of place on fresh water. We also found a solitary boat-billed heron perched in the tules along the lake's edge, and we got very excited when we heard a ruddy crake along the shoreline. We made several unsuccessful attempts to get a look at this secretive bird, even though it was walking about in the thick grasses almost under our feet. I decided to try a trick I had read about.

"Johnathan," I said, "Let's walk back and forth to create a narrow open corridor in the grass, and see if we can entice it to cross the open area." That is what we did, and we imitated its call several times, the crake finally ran across the open area, and we had a quick but satisfying look.

Mangrove vireos were surprisingly common within the forest edges near the lakes. We also found an eye-ringed flatbill. At first, I thought it was a large *Empidonax* flycatcher, but in a few seconds, I realized I was watching a very green bird with a very broad and flat bill. "Johnathan, here is an eye-ringed flatbill, a new trip bird. Come see it." We both had a very good look at this Mexican flycatcher.

At dinner that evening, we talked about our day and that we wished Gretchen and Marian were available for another night. I asked Johnathan, "Are you familiar with German women? Gretchen certainly knew how to please me. My take away from that experience is that they are more honest and straight forward than any of the American women I have dated."

"I agree with you. I asked Marian if she had a boyfriend back home and she told me she did and was planning to marry soon after she returns home. I asked her if she had been a virgin, and she said, yes, I wanted to have experience before marrying."

"I wonder if they met us for that express purpose. Women are strange in a number of ways."

"Robert," Johnathan said, "we are only a few miles from Tulum, a Mayan site along the Caribbean Coast. Why don't we drive over there tomorrow and stay at Cobá another night? I would like to see that site; I understand that Tulum is very different from the ruins we have been visiting the last several days."

"I have no problem with that. Plus, I doubt that we will find a better place to stay than Cobá. However, maybe instead of returning to Cobá, how about heading up the coast from Tulum to see some of the coastal sites? And I would also love to visit Cozumel Island. There are two endemic birds there, the Cozumel thrasher and Cozumel vireo. Plus, I am told that Cozumel also is the mostly likely place to see a stripe-headed tanager."

After checking out of Villas Arqueologicas, we drove the 26 miles from Cobá to Tulum in less than an hour. Tulum is located on a cliff overlooking the Caribbean, a fascinating setting. The brochure we purchased at Tulum informed us that it was a Mayan site dating from about 700 A.D. and functioned continuously until the arrival of the Spaniards. The brochure also stated that "Tulum means wall or trench in the Mayan language, and it also was known as Zama, meaning 'City of Dawn,' because it faces the sunrise." Tulum was one of the last large Mayan cities to collapse, largely due to Old World diseases introduced by the Spaniards.

The principal feature at Tulum is a 19-foot thick wall that encircles the city. According to the brochure, the wall averages 16 feet high, and is 1,250 feet on the west side and 560 feet along the two sides. It also asserts that most of the Mayan inhabitants lived outside the walls, leaving the interior for the royal class and ceremonial structures, including the 20-foot high El Castillo.

"Although I can understand the walls that probably served as barriers to invaders, why such a non-imposing castle?" I asked.

"Maybe because the priests lacked management skills to dominate the workers."

"But the width of the wall seems to defy that idea."

In addition to El Castillo, we found an even smaller structure at the very foot of El Castillo that was identified as the Temple of Frescoes and had served as an observatory. The local guard explained that the Mayans used that temple for "tracking the movements of the sun." That didn't make much sense to us, but because the guard spoke very little English, we were unable to learn more. We did, however, enjoy the time we spent at Tulum. It was a gorgeous day and the ruins provided a very different setting from the ruins we had already seen.

Afterwards, we drove up the coast to Playa del Carmen, where we found a room in a coastal hotel. The next morning, we boarded the ferry *Itzam* which three times daily crosses the 12-mile channel between Playa del Carmen and Cozumel's village-port of San Miguel. The crossing took just under one hour, but surprisingly, it was a trip that did not meet our expectations.

The waters that surround Cozumel are ranked among the world's most outstanding areas for diving, but despite the beauty of the waters and their incredible clarity, marine life was scarce. We saw no fish within the crystal-clear waters, and the birdlife was minimal. We recorded only a few royal terns during the entire crossing. That paucity of birdlife over open tropical waters is fairly typical; warm tropical waters do not support as much plankton, the tiny animals and plants that provide a food base for larger species, as do colder ocean waters. In a sense, the lack of birdlife around the island was in direct contrast to its name.

'Cozumel' is derived from the Mayan word *Cuzamil*, which has been translated to mean Island of Swallows. Swallows were completely absent during our brief visit, although we did see a number of Vaux's swifts, a swallow-like bird that is more closely related to hummingbirds than swallows.

"Seeing no swallows," Johnathan said, "Maybe they should have name Cozumel "Island of Swifts" instead."

We had intended to rent a car to drive ourselves around the island, but the man at the local office told us that none were available, but that we could secure a taxi at one of the stores in town. We hadn't walked very far when we were approached by a gentleman in an old and rather run-down sedan. He informed us that he was willing to take us on a tour of the island. We thanked him and said that we were not interested in a tour but in visiting the El Rey ruins and also finding a few of the local birds. He said that his nephew was the local bird expert and he could arrange a tour by his nephew.

"Please get in the car and we will find my nephew; he can take you wherever you want to go. He has taken many others out to see birds," he said.

The 1957 Chevrolet bore lots of dents and scratches, but we decided that a driver who could also act as a guide to the best birding localities, as well as the ruins, would be well worth our while. So, we gave in, jumped into the car, and off we drove to find our 'expert' guide.

We drove from one end of San Miguel to the other and back again looking for the nephew, whom we never did find. At our fourth or fifth stop, we picked up another relative, however. His name was Juan, and we were never sure about his relationship to the old man.

In the meantime, we began to realize that the day was fast slipping away. After about a dozen stops, we decided it was time to find another taxi, but when we announced this, our driver immediately informed us, without even a glance at Juan, that Juan was to be our driver and was ready to go. The conversation that followed between the two was not very clear, despite Johnathan's knowledge of Spanish. We were never sure whether Juan had known this all along or whether he was surprised as we were. Nevertheless, we decided it would be easier and faster to go ahead with these arrangements than to seek out another taxi and driver in downtown San Miguel. And in the long run, Juan was very helpful, and he knew the island very well.

During our downtown tour, while searching for the nephew, despite the repetition, we did record several birds as we progressed from one stop to the next. We found an amazing number of North American warblers and at one stop, next to a large weedy lot, we coaxed a black catbird into the open.

The San Gervacio ruins are located on the northern portion of the island, and it took us less than an hour's drive to reach the entrance. After asking Juan to wait for us, we purchased our tickets and a brochure and began to walk about the compound. Almost immediately we were disappointed with the ruins, as very few of the structures had been restored. We did learn that the site had once been a hub of worship of the goddess Ix Chal, an age-old deity of childbirth, fertility, medicine, and weaving. How that combination worked together was left to our imagination.

"Johnathan," I said, "I see a stone arch that seems to be one of the few remaining structures. Let's take a look." While we were approaching the stone arch, we saw a huge iguana lying at the top.

Suddenly, a guide appeared seemingly out of nowhere. In very broken English he said "Welcome to San Gervasio. You like the arch?"

"Actually, we were admiring the huge iguana," I said.

"Sí, San Gervasio is also a refugia for grandee lizards. They are protected here. They are very rare elsewhere on Cozumel."

Johnathan spoke up. "We like iguanas, and we are glad they are protected here. But can you tell us about the ruins?"

The guard introduced himself as Carmón and began to tell us about the ruins. He mostly told us what we already had learned, but he did say that the ruins were most active from 1200 to about 1600, when they were abandoned. He also added that Pre-Columbian women made a pilgrimage to San Gervasio at least once in their lifetime.

"I suppose it is like the many Christians who make pilgrimages to Jerusalem and Rome," I said.

It wasn't long before we lost interest in the ruins and returned to our taxi and Juan. By this time, it was late in the afternoon, and realizing that we would have much better luck finding our birds during the morning hours, we had Juan take us to a hotel in San Miguel. Once we secured a room, we arranged with Juan to pick us up early the next morning to take us where we could find our birds.

He seemed very happy with that arrangement, and when we asked him about a good nearby restaurant, he recommended the Cozumel Hotel, where we were staying.

In the morning, when we walked into the restaurant for breakfast, we found Juan waiting for us. Before long, the three of us were en route to find our target birds. Our first stop was at a small but beautiful freshwater lake, called Chancanab Lagoon, only four miles out of town. Juan said that the lagoon was connected to the sea by underground channels. The crystal-clear water seemed to be moving in no direction, and since no outlet was evident, we believed his story.

"Juan," I said, "Stop here for a few minutes and let us see what birds might be in and about the lagoon."

We immediately found a least grebe, tricolored heron, several blue-winged teal, and a number of common moorhens. We also were attracted to an unfamiliar song emanating from the adjacent vegetation. We soon coaxed the songster out of its hiding place. "Robert, it's a golden warbler, one of our target birds." And soon we found several others in the vegetation along the edge of the lagoon.

Our route that morning took us along a large mangrove forest, and we stopped several times to see what we could coax into the open. We did find several North America warblers and vireos. As we continued along the outer beach drive, our taxi suddenly died, and came to a coasting stop. I guessed that we were almost halfway around the 50-mile loop drive.

At first, Juan insisted that it was a mechanical problem that he could fix, and he spent almost an hour peering under the hood trying to discover the difficulty. Since none of the various dashboard gauges worked, they were of no help. Soon we began to wonder whether or not the car was merely out of gasoline, and after a while Johnathan made that suggestion. With that, Juan suddenly struck off down the road on his own to find help, and we were left to ourselves. Within the hour he was back. Somehow, he had found his 'brother,' acquired a large can of gasoline, and had returned to save the day. On our way around the other half of the loop, we watched for where he might have found his brother and acquired the gasoline but saw nothing that could give us a hint of what had occurred.

Johnathan finally asked, "Juan, does your brother live nearby? Did he have extra gasoline?"

The only answer we got was: "My brother was nearby, and we had to borrow gasoline from a friend."

While waiting for gasoline, Johnathan and I had walked up and down the road searching for whatever birds might be present. Most abundant were palm warblers, which were readily called up by squeaking sounds, and we also found a lone Cozumel thrasher, one of our key target birds. It struck me as rather dull and a smaller version of a brown thrasher.

When we finally continued along the loop road, a couple miles before entering San Miguel we came upon a patch of woody vegetation, to which we decided to explore, hoping for a Cozumel vireo. We knew that this vireo preferred woodland, but until then, we had not seen habitat that would be appropriate.

"Stop here, please," I said. "This habitat looks good for the vireo." Within another 20 minutes we had called up a pair of Cozumel vireos. Within another 20 minutes we had located four others. We had hit the Cozumel vireo jackpot! However, Juan seemed to take credit for us finding our bird.

Since we had found both of Cozumel's avian endemics, we decided to spend the remainder of the day trying to find a stripe-headed tanager. "Juan," I said, "Where might we find a stripe-headed tanager?" And without any hesitation, he answered, "At the jardin." And suddenly Juan was a new man, as if he had been waiting all day for us to ask for his help. And just as suddenly he turned off the main roadway into a narrow, wooded lane that led into a large and very active nursery. We climbed out of the car and within another ten minutes, I found our bird.

'Johnathan," I called. "Come here; I've found our bird." I had first detected the bird from its call, a drawn-out "seep" that led me to where I had a great look at it. Johnathan and I followed it about for several minutes before we realized that it was time to head back to town and something to eat. It had been a long, somewhat unusual day, but successful nevertheless.

CHAPTER 6

CANCÚN TO VALLADOLID

OUR DAY ON Cozumel had been successful; we had visited some new ruins and had found three target birds.

In the morning, before boarding the ferry to return to the mainland, we sat in the restaurant eating breakfast and talking about what we should do during the day ahead. We had passed several ruins on our drive from Tulum to Playa del Carmen and the ferry to Cozumel, and we talked about turning back to see those sites or going north toward Cancún.

"I think I would prefer heading north and seeing a few ruins in the Cancún area rather than going south," I said. "Although Xcaret is a seaport site very near Playa del Carmen, it is still active, so I would guess that those ruins would not truly represent the Mayan period. I would prefer going north."

"I think I agree," Johnathan said. "We know that there are a couple ruins very near Cancún, but I am concerned about getting too far into the city. Cancún, from what I have read, has become too touristy for me. I hope we can remain on the edge."

We boarded the ferry and soon were back on the mainland and driving northward toward Cancún. Our plan for the day was to visit both El Rey and San Miguelito, and because they are relatively small sites that could be seen in a short time, we would then drive on to Valladolid for the night.

San Miguelito is a small Mayan ruin located on the grounds of the Cancún Mayan Museum. San Miguelito was built to honor the Mayan god

Chock. According to the Yucatan guidebook, the site had been inhabited from 1250 to 1550, and contains 40 structures, although only a few have been restored to any degree. The largest is the Chock Palace, a 26-foot high structure with five stories and a stairwell with a carving of the god Chock into every stone. The adjacent Dragon Complex includes numerous hieroglyphs carved into the stones. We spent a few minutes examining the hieroglyphs, but they were so badly weathered that it was almost impossible to identify most of the figures. We were, however, able to identify a bird of some sort, and another was clearly a crocodile. We would have spent more time there, but the museum was closed, so we drove to the nearby El Rey ruins.

The El Rey ruins, we learned, had been occupied from 1200 to 1500 and were part of a Mayan trade route and a fishing center. According to the brochure, it was once known as "Kin Ich Ahay Bonil," Mayan for King of the Solar Countenance. The compound includes a total of 47 structures, including four large buildings and lots of platforms and bases. We found that most of the columns were worn to the point that we were unable to see any of the hieroglyphs. The brochure also stated that El Rey was the burial grounds for royalty as well as an astronomical education center.

"You would think that, if this site truly was an astronomical center, the tower should have been reconstructed to exemplify that fact," Johnathan said.

"But, instead," I said, "The El Rey ruins that I will long remember are not the ruins per se, but the incredible number of huge iguanas that are everywhere. I can't believe the number and size of these iguanas."

Many iguanas lay sunning themselves on the ruin walls, even on the walls that have fallen over and lay on the ground. Some of the smaller iguanas were even lying on top of the larger ones. Never before had either of us seen so many iguanas in such close quarters.

I eventually remarked, "I wonder if the early Mayans ate iguana. I wonder how iguana stew, with plenty of jalapeños, would taste."

"Maybe we can find iguana stew or steaks at our next restaurant?"

"I do know that early sailors introduced iguanas into many of the Caribbean Islands. It was their way of providing food for shipwrecked sailors."

"After seeing this mob of iguanas, I can tell you where they acquired their iguanas."

We did not spend much time at the Cancún ruins and were en route to Valladolid by late morning. We had decided not to remain in the Concún area, and by the time we stopped to eat, we were at Leona Vicerio, a very small town along the highway. From the outside, the Vicerio Restaurant looked rather old and run down, but the inside was very neat and clean, and the lady who waited on us spoke some English.

Johnathan asked her what she would recommend for two travelers, and she said that her *carne guisada* was ready and that all the locals claimed that her *carne guiasada* was the best in the Yucatan. Johnathan said, "*Carne guiasada* in Mexican beef stew, and I, for one, want that."

The senora was pleased, and she soon placed a huge bowl of *carne guiasada*, along with pieces of homemade bread and butter, in front of each of us. She stood back and watched as we took our first bite. It was delicious, although a little spicy for me. But Johnathan said that it was "perfecto." Senora Aguilar, as she had introduced herself, looked extremely pleased. Before we had finished our stew, she asked where we were going, and how long had we been traveling? Johnathan told her that we primarily were visiting several ruins and that we planned on staying at Valladolid overnight and seeing Ek' Balan tomorrow. He added, "Sooner or later, we plan to see Palenque and Uxmal. Have you had an opportunity to visit those sites?"

"Sí, when I was a girl my parents took my sister and me to see many of the ruins. But now my elderly father can no longer travel, and we must stay here until he is better."

It wasn't until then that we noticed an elderly gentleman in a wheelchair in the doorway to the kitchen. He seemed to be paying close attention to our conversation. In another minute, Senora Aguilar added that her father needed to go to a doctor in Valladolid, but she was unable to take him because she was caring for her very sick mother in another room and could not leave her.

We were unsure what to say, but Sonora Aguilar said, "I believe that you are honorable people and can be trusted. If you are going to Valladolid, would you consider taking my father? You will be going right by the hospital as you enter town, and it would take you very little time. If you would, I would be so very thankful. And my sister can take my place here tomorrow, so I could drive into the hospital to bring him back if he is able. God bless you for your help!"

We looked at each other and at the same time, said "Yes, we would be glad to do that."

"Thank you, thank you. God will bless you."

We had a little problem getting Senor Aguilar into the back seat of the car and, in order to also take his wheelchair, we had to do a little repacking. It took us a good part of an hour before we were ready to go. Senor Aguilar did not say a word while we were getting settled, but once we were on the road, he talked almost constantly.

He told us much of his life history, from being a boy in Chemac where he played baseball for the local team, to joining the Mexican navy during the Second World War, to returning to Valladolid to live with his daughter. He was aware of what we had been doing in the Yucatan, and he said that his favorite ruin was Ek' Balan. He mentioned that his family lived near there for many years. He also told us that, after he returned from the navy, he had volunteered to help with the excavations of several of the Ek' Balan structures. Suddenly, he was silent.

After a few minutes I looked back at him, and he was slumped over in the backseat as if he had fallen asleep. "Johnathan," I said. "I guess he is asleep. Do you want to check?"

With that, Johnathan turned around in the seat and said, "Senor Aguilar, are you OK?" There was no response, but Johnathan said that he could tell he was breathing.

We were by then entering Valladolid, and just ahead was a sign for the hospital. I immediately drove up to the entrance, and Johnathan jumped out of the car and ran inside. Within seconds, he returned with an attendant. Once the attendant saw our passenger, whom he seemed to know, he immediately began to examine him. "Senor Aguilar, stay with me. I will take you in, so we can examine you more." Within a few minutes, he hurried back into the hospital and returned with an assistant and a gurney. They lifted Senor Aguilar onto the gurney and wheeled him inside.

We sat there in the car not knowing what to do. "We need to go inside and tell the doctor how we happened to be with him." While I parked the car at a designated space, Johnathan entered the hospital and found the doctor who had first attended Mr. Aguilar. By the time I entered the hospital, I found Johnathan talking with one of the other doctors. The doctor explaining that Mr. Aguilar had been ill for many months and had not come into town to a doctor as had been recommended. "Now," he said, "I am afraid Senor Aguilar may be very ill. I will contact his cousin, who lives nearby, and ask him to contact his daughters."

Johnathan told the doctor how we happened to bring Senor Aguilar to the hospital and what had occurred during our drive into town. They talked for several more minutes before Johnathan said, "It seems to me that there is nothing more we can do. Why don't we find a motel in town, get settled, and after dinner, we can return to see how he is." I agreed that we could do nothing more, so we left the hospital and drove further into town to find a room for the night.

We found a room at the Ecotel Quinta Reyes, reasonably close to Highway 295, which goes north from town toward a couple of ruins we planned to visit. After dinner we returned to the hospital to see how Senor Aguilar was doing. As we walked into the waiting-room we found Senora Aguilar, three daughters, and a number of other relations, including cousins, an aunt and an uncle. We never did learn how they all were able to come to the hospital in such record time. We were introduced to everyone, and with each handshake was a hearty *muchas gracias* for the help that we had provided. Two of the daughters, our approximate age, thanked us profusely. We honestly did not think that we had done as much as they seemed to think we had done.

When we asked about Senor Aguilar's condition, we were told that the doctor had said that he had had a stroke, and because he had reached the hospital and care soon enough, they predicted that he would live and recover enough to go home after a few days. The entire family believed that his recovery was due to Johnathan and me for getting him to the hospital in record time. We remained with the family for about an hour before excusing ourselves and began to leave. But Maria and Margaréte walked us outside and asked about our plans to visit some of the ruins. "We have worked at Ek' Balam in the past and know that area very well. We would be honored by an opportunity to be your guides."

Although neither of us wanted their help simply because we had been helpful with their father, we certainly did not turn down their assistance.

Maria said, "We seldom have an opportunity to talk with a native American, and since we are both learning English in school, being able to talk with you would be a great deal of help in learning your language."

"Where do you go to school? Is there a local school in Valladolid?"

"Yes, there is what is called a 'junior college' in America. We plan to go on to university afterwards."

I realized that here were two very bright and lovely girls, although in retrospect, they were more than just girls.

We later guessed their ages at 17 and 16.

After some time, talking about their life and answering questions about our journey, we parted, they returned to the hospital waiting-room, and we drove to our hotel for the night. Before departing, however, we arranged to meet them in the morning at the hospital. "But," they added, "We hope our father will be well. If he is not recovered well enough, we cannot join you."

By morning, when we met them at the hospital, the whole Aguilar family, including Senor Aguilar, was sitting in the waiting room. The doctors had told him that he had a very mild stroke and must remain at the hospital for two or three more days. He looked perfectly fine to me, but I knew that a stroke, even a very mild stroke, was not an illness one ignored.

After talking with the family, we left with the two women for our trip to Ek' Balam. And when we arrived, they seemed to know almost everyone we encountered, from the lady selling tickets to the ruins to the two guards. Both knew a lot about the ruins, and they began their interpretation of the site even before we had entered.

Ek' Balam, which means "glorious jaguar" in Mayan, dates from 700 to 1000 A.D. and contains 45 structures.

The entire 24-acre compound is surrounded by two concentric walls that end at impassably steep-sided sink holes.

"Maria," I asked, "Were the inhabitants at war with their neighbors? Why the extensive double walls?"

"I am told that many of the cities were at war with other cities during that period. I am also told that Ek' Balam was the center of the Mayan kingdom, and they constantly had to defend themselves against cities attempting to usurp their authority."

As we wandered around the compound, I was impressed with the number of structures that had been either completely or partially restored. For instance, the entrance arch had been built over the entrance road leading into the city. Most impressive was the Oval Palace. "This structure contained burial relicts, and it is said that its alignment is connected to cosmological ceremonies," Margaréte said.

I added, "According to the brochure, the walls contain 46 glyphs, which are scattered among numerous murals, and the glyphs have been described as "master works." Although most were barely discernable, we found one that was in the obvious shape of a deer.

We found that only the center of Ek' Balam had been fully excavated, but large partially restored platforms lined the interior walls, and roads stemmed off the center in four cardinal directions.

We continued our visit, inspecting one structure after another. The largest structure was a temple in which archeologists had found the tomb of Ikit Kan Le'k Tok,' which has a doorway in the shape of a monster. "Look at that," I said, "It looks like a huge mouth, maybe depicting a jaguar."

The ballcourt had been totally restored, even the stone rings at each end. The structures at each end of the Acropolis were great platforms that served as major plazas, each with a temple on one corner. We also found a carved stela that depicted a ruler.

"This whole compound is extremely impressive," Johnathan said. "I read that the Mayans had developed steam baths."

We wandered over to what the brochure called "steam baths," but they had not been restored. "How was the water heated," I asked.

Johnathan answered that the brochure claimed that fires were laid directly underneath to heat the water. "I find that impractical. Can you imagine someone sitting on hot rocks?"

"There must have been more to the heating process. Most early people heated rocks that were then placed in the water."

By the time we left the Ek' Balam ruins, it was time to eat. Margaréte told us that her grandmother lived nearby, and she had invited us all to go there for lunch. When we arrived, her grandmother seemed to be extremely happy to have unexpected guests. While she was preparing our food, we were taken in the backyard, where there was a sizable garden. There were rows of vegetables, all looking amazingly healthy. I could not help but wonder if grandmother had help or if she was the sole gardener.

When Johnathan asked her about her garden, she said that she was the lone gardener and that she sold much of her produce to neighbors and to a small nearby store. I never did see a store, but we were more than satisfied with what she provided that day for our lunch. In fact, that lunch was one of the few that contained mostly vegetables rather than meat. She also provided us with spicy beans and tortillas. Johnathan and I later talked about that meal and how unusual it was to us. We agreed that it was excellent!

The remainder of the day we spent returning to town and to the hospital where we checked on Senor Aguilar. We found the Aguilar family still in the waiting room and seemingly in a good mood. Between the time we visited the hospital that morning and our return, the Aguilar family had about doubled in size. More cousins, aunts, uncles and friends had all gathered to see Senor Aguilar, who appeared to be the family patriarch. He was happy to see his two daughters and once again thanked Johnathan and me for all that we had done.

After visiting with the happy group for more than an hour, we bid our farewells, especially thanking Maria and Margaréte for their tour of El' Balam. They walked us out to our car where we again said our farewells, and they hurried back inside to be with their happy family.

We returned to our hotel, where we ate dinner and talked about our day and the remarkable family we had met.

CHAPTER 7

CHETUMAL: KOHUNLICH AND CALAKMUL

THE NEXT MORNING, we drove to the hospital to check on Senor Aguilar. As we entered the waiting-room, almost all the Aguilar family was still there. A couple of the younger folks were still asleep, laid out on the floor without covers. Others were sitting around on the few available chairs or on the floor against a wall. We were told that Senor Aguilar was still in his room and that his condition had improved even more since we had seen him last night. Maria and Margaréte gave us a hug, and when they learned that we came by to check on Senor Aguilar before leaving town, they seemed truly sad.

We soon were on our way to Palenque, or so we thought. Our intended route was to take us out of the state of Yucatan, into Quintana Roo and past Felipe Carillo Puerto, south to Los Lemones and southwest past Chetumal and into Campeche, then west toward the Gulf of Mexico. But even before we got to Felipe Carillo Puerto, Johnathan, who had been reading the Yucatan guidebook while I was driving, said, "Let's stop overnight at Chetumal. There are a number of ruins in that area and we should check them out." Since his suggestion also provided opportunities to see some Mexican birds I had not yet seen, I agreed.

We stopped for lunch at Felipe Carrillo Puerto, a town of about 26,000 people, and soon found a restaurant that looked busy with locals. We entered the restaurant and were led to a table and asked what we wanted to drink; we both asked for orange soda. The menu contained a good variety of options, but Johnathan said, "I don't see Senora Aguilar's *carne guiasada;* that was really good! I wonder what the specialty of Café Felipe Carillo might be. But we never did ask the lady that waited on us, as she automatically brought us a huge bowl of salsa and chips and some fish sticks. We ate our fill without ordering anything more. The total cost of that lunch was less than five dollars for the two of us.

Our next stop was Chetumal, a city of about 150,000 people. Chetumal is situated at the southeastern corner of Quintana Roo, on the Bay of Coruzal, one of the finest bays on the Yucatan. According to the guidebook, the first Spaniards to reach the area were shipwrecked and enslaved by the Mayans; they later were freed by Cortez and served as interpreters. One of the captives married a Mayan princess and fought against the Spaniards for many years.

"It is interesting to me how, in those years, captives and captors often joined forces against a mutual enemy," I said. "And how often," I added, "did one or more of the captives became significant members of their new society."

"I agree. But you know the same relationships occur today. Look at all the slaves that were brought to the Americas who eventually blended into the environment. Some of those individuals came from royalty in their own country. I realize that some, maybe many of those slaves, were gradually considered members of the upper class." By the time we found a hotel, it was late afternoon. Before eating, we decided to walk around town and take in the local atmosphere. The downtown plaza was pretty much the same as what we had seen in many other Mexican cities. Local folks were walking about or sitting on benches talking about whatever was on their minds.

We found a bench along the side of the plaza, where we sat and watched the people. On the next bench were two women who also were people-watching. Before long Johnathan had struck up a conservation with them; they seemed very happy to be talking with someone from 'far-off' America.

When Johnathan asked them about the best restaurant in the area, they recommended the Palenque, right down the street. When we decided it was time to eat, the two women – Reba and Jóse – were invited to join us. The four of us walked to the Palenque and were soon eating a dinner that I thought was excellent.

"Johnathan," I said, "This is the best food I have eaten since Cobá. Thank you so much, Jóse, for recommending the Palenque."

During the course of the meal, we learned that Reba and Jóse were attending the University of Quintana Roo. When asked where they were from, they said they were from Coabas, a little town to the west. They asked us where we were from, and when Johnathan said Miami and I said St. Croix, they asked where St. Croix is; they apparently already knew that Miami was in the state of Florida.

Although I did not speak much Spanish and neither of the women spoke much English, I think that they got a general idea of that St. Croix is an island in the Caribbean Sea. Johnathan filled in some necessary details.

Reba asked, "What are you doing in Quintana Roo?" Johnathan explained that we were visiting several Mayan ruins all though the Yucatan. Both women suddenly got excited, and Reba said, "We are studying the Mayan civilization at school. Although we know Kohunlich, because it is nearby, I would love to see many more of the ruins." She added: "And not too far beyond Kohunlich is Calakmul; my brother works there. If you go there, you must meet my brother. He is a guard, and I know he would be very happy to tell you about his ruins."

The remainder of our conversation consisted of various things that young people talk about when getting acquainted. And before long it was time to go our own ways. However, before we left the restaurant, Jóse, who seemed to be partial to me, suggested that we meet again tomorrow evening. She said that she would like to hear about our day at the ruins.

The next day, we chose to visit Kohunlich first and, due perhaps to Jóse's friendly invitation to spend another evening with them, we decided to stay in Chetumal another night. En route to Kohunlich, we talked about Reba and Jóse. We guessed that they were 17 or 18 years old, and both seemed knowledgeable about the nearby ruins.

We found that Kohunlich was an isolated site that was well maintained and provided a good example of the later Mayan period. The ruins themselves cover an area of less than one square mile, but a portion was built on a low hill, which provided an excellent view of the surrounding landscape.

When we asked about Senor Ramérez, Jóse's brother, we were told he was not there that day. But another of the guards, Ricárdo Gómez, was willing to spend the day as our interpreter. He asked if we knew Senor Ramérez, and we told him we did not, but had met his daughter. Ricárdo immediately expressed his admiration of Jóse, saying that he hoped to marry her one day. He added, "I have already asked her father for her hand, but he has not yet approved. I pray that he will very soon."

Ricárdo did an excellent job as our interpreter. One of the first pyramids we saw was the Pyramid of the Masks. "This is the most distinctive structure at Kohunlich," he said. "Notice the staircase. It is flanked by eight different five-foot-tall stucco masks which represent the Mayan sun god. The upper part of the pyramid contains four tombs at different levels."

From the base of the pyramid, we could see the upper levels and visualize the four chambers. "When the pyramid was first excavated, did the archeologists find human remains in the tombs?" I asked.

"No, I am told that, although the pyramid looked untouched, grave robbers had already stolen all the artifacts from the tombs. Some of those stolen artifacts can be seen at the Cairo Museum in Egypt."

"The Cairo Museum? Why not the Mexican National Museum? That is where all of the valuable Mexican artifacts should be maintained."

"I agree with you, but during the days when so many of our structures were being excavated, many key artifacts were sold to other museums; that was the way Mexico was able to fund the work."

The remainder of the day was spent walking from one structure to another. Each had its own story, and I was impressed with Ricárdo's knowledge and his ability as an interpreter. We finally bid him farewell and drove back to Chetumal. As we were leaving, he said, "Please, give my very best to Jóse. I love her so!"

Although I wondered about his comment and openness, Johnathan said that most Mexican men he has known are very open with their feelings. "Ricárdo certainly let us know where he stood about Jóse."

By the time we arrived back in Chetumal, it was late afternoon. We showered and dressed into something other than our field cloths, and drove into town for dinner. We parked a couple blocks from the restaurant, and walked past the plaza to the restaurant. We found Reba and Jóse waiting for us. After some small talk, the four of us walked to the Palenque for dinner. As soon as we sat down, they wanted to know how our day at Kohunlich had gone, and Jóse asked if we had met her brother.

"No," Johnathan answered, "he was not there, but we did spend the day with Ricárdo, and he ask us to tell you hello. He also told us that he wants to marry you. Is that your plan?"

Jóse seemed embarrassed and even upset. "He has asked my father if he can marry me, but I am not ready. I want to finish school. I do not want to have a family before I have a degree. My father knows this, so I can only hope he does not give in to Robérto."

"Does your father understand that you are not ready?"

"If he does, I am afraid that he is far more interested in becoming part of Robérto's expansive family. They are very well-to-do, and I am afraid that wealth means more to him than his daughter's education. I can only hope that I can finish my schooling."

Reba added, "In Mexico, women our age are often forced to marry whomever our fathers believe will most benefit his family. It often is not who we would prefer."

By the time we had finished our meals, and after some additional conversation, it was rather late and time to go our separate ways. We told Jóse and Reba that we planned to leave Chetumal in the morning and head for Calakmul, our next ruins, and not return to Chetumal. Our parting was a little sad, as we had enjoyed our association with both Jóse and Reba.

Back at our room, Johnathan said, "It is sad that a daughter in Mexico has so little opportunity to go against her father. When daddy decides what is best for his daughter, there is seldom a different result."

"I wonder what the final solution might be. Many young women attend school primarily to meet the right man. Maybe Jóse would be better off giving in to her father. But, if she is not already in love with Robérto, that would not be her best option."

"I agree, but Mexican families too often follow the age-old concept of doing what is expected by the parents rather than what they want for themselves."

"I can only hope that in the long-run Jóse will find happiness."

By morning, our primary attention was focused on seeing our next ruins, Calakmul. We reached Calakmul at mid-day, and we were hungry. We found a small restaurant near the entrance to the ruins, and within a few more minutes we were eating. The waitress was very friendly, and she and Johnathan were soon involved with a long discussion about where we were from and what we were doing in Mexico. Although she was old enough to be my mother, she seemed to love her two American customers. Afterwards, Johnathan told me that she had suggested that she would be available to both of us that night. She had mentioned that she would do anything to go to America.

"It sounds to me," I said, "that she has seen too many American movies. Did she think we could just take her with us and hide her in a suitcase when we returned to the U.S."

"No, she even suggested that she would be willing to marry one of us and could then go with us as a wife."

"That is one crazy lady! Do you think she was serious, or was she just kidding around?"

"I think she was very serious. You know, we have met some unusual people on our trip. This is one of the strangest, but the Aguilar family was one of the very best. I wonder what else we will find before we get back to the states?"

We were amazed at Calakmul; it was a huge site. I wondered why it was not featured in our guidebook; it was barely mentioned. It did state that Calakmul was within an International Biosphere Reserve, and that it was located within an extensive rain forest. That forest, which appeared to be pristine, was obvious long before we reached the site. From our car, the forest looked thick with many trees and lianas.

"Maybe we can find some trails to explore for bird specialties," I said.

"I know that there are numerous Yucatan specialties that we could find. Let's check out the Calakmul ruins first and maybe explore the adjacent forest afterwards."

We bought a brochure at the entrance and were soon wandering about the compound. Johnathan, on reading the brochure, said, "Calakmul is the single largest of all the Mayan sites, covering forty-two square miles and containing 6,750 uncovered structures. It also suggests that there are many more to be excavated." He added: "Calakmul once had a population of 50,000 souls. And it states that Calakmul in the Mayan language means "City of two adjacent pyramids."

"I had no idea about the significant of this site. If all this is true, I would rank Calakmul right along with Cobá and Tikal. And speaking of Tikal, we might want to think about visiting that site as well. It probably will require a flight, but it might be worth our time and funds."

"Look, off to the left next to that pyramid, there is an ocellated turkey. What a bird!"

Sure enough, as we scoped the grounds, we found more than a dozen of these large birds. Each had a multicolored body, with a greenish chest and back, broad rusty wing bands, and a naked blue head with red eyes. As we got closer, we could hear their strange gobbling, a nasal pumping sound that accerated in speed. "Wow, seeing these turkeys makes the entire visit to Calakmul worthwhile!"

"I can't believe the number of turkeys we are seeing, just wandering around with no fear of predators or people. I knew that the species is native to the Yucatan, but I didn't expect to see so many and so close-up. A real treat!"

As we continued our wandering, we stopped at Pyramid 2, which according to the brochure, was 148 feet in height, the tallest in Mexico. The site also has 130 stelae, but when we examined a couple, we found that they were very well worn, and it was difficult to identify any of the carvings. The site also contains several temples, two acropolises, and a ballcourt.

Reading the brochure, Johnathan said, "Calakmul leaders were called "Serpent Head Polity," because their use of a serpent head by their chief. It also states that Calakmul was the most important of all the Mayan ruins."

"I now look forward to our visits to Chichén and Uxmal to see how those ruins compare with these at Calakmul." As much as we enjoyed the ruins and recognized their importance in Mayan history, we kept looking at the birds that we found within the compound and along the edge; we were anxious to get inside the forest. The Yucatan guidebook, primarily described the ruins, but it also mentioned the forest, which is considered one of the last of the great Yucatan rain forests. It also stated that Mexico is host to ten percent of all plants and animals in the world and that the Calakmul Reserve contains 400 to 500 jaguars.

"Would you believe the number of jaguars," I said. "Maybe we will be lucky enough to see one of those huge cats. I would love to see a jaguar, but maybe at a distance."

Before long we were walking about in the forest. Although we did not see a jaguar during the more than three hours we spent in the forest interior, we did find fresh tracks on at least two occasions. The birdlife was amazing! We recorded a total of 86 species in the short time available, and more than half of those were new to our trip list.

The avian highlights that day were two raptors: gray-headed kite and short-tailed hawk. The kite was an adult with a pearly-gray head, a slaty back, pale underparts, and dark brown eyes. It remained on the upper branches of a tall tree, but flew off soon after we had a short but good look. We had a much longer look at the short-tailed hawk. It stayed still long enough for us to see its dark brown upperparts, including a dusky malar patch. Then it took off and circled about us for two or three minutes before flying away. It called out several times; its call was a persistent scream, like "kyeeahh, kyeeahh."

But despite of our desire to spend more time in the Calakmul forest and area, we left before dark and drove on to Francisco Escarega, located at the junction of Highways 261 and 307. By the time we found a hotel and freshened up, we were starving. The hotel had a decent restaurant, so we ate there and discussed our next adventure.

Once again, the idea of visiting Tikal in nearby Guatemala became the major part of our discussion. By this time, we both were pretty excited about that idea, and we decided to check the airport in the morning about flights.

Once we returned to our room, we talked about Tikal for several more hours. And after turning in, I had a difficult time sleeping. My mind was primed for Tikal.

CHAPTER 8

TIKAL

THE NEXT DAY, after breakfast, we drove to the airport to find out about a flight to Tikal. We learned that there was an Aerovias flight to Tikal at 11:30 a.m. We bought tickets and, since we had a couple hours to wait, we walked around the outer edge of the runway to see what birds might be present. Except for several white-collared seedeaters, we did not see any species that we had not seen earlier.

We boarded our flight on time, and we landed at Flores, Guatemala, in about an hour. Because we did not have a car to drive the 60 miles to Tikal, we found a taxi that would take us to Tikal for twenty dollars. When we arrived at Tikal, we discovered that the Jaguar Inn was full. After a long discussion with the clerk, we were allowed to stay in one of the cottages that was being remodeled.

Although it was far from being a comfortable room as previously experienced, it did provide us a place to sleep, and we were able to have our meals in the nearby dining area. By then it was dinner time, and we were unable to spend any time at the ruins or to check on what birdlife might be available.

The meal that evening was only so-so, but we did meet several other folks who were there to see the ruins, as well as two young ladies, about our ages, who were there to see the ruins and also to find birds. After introducing ourselves, we discovered that they were graduate students from the University of California at Berkeley, on a holiday after completing their senior year studying environmental education. Our friendship was almost instantaneous. Carol and Katherine were beautiful women who were very personable. Our conservations in the dining room lasted for a couple of hours, but we finally left the restaurant and walked to our rooms. They had one of the new cottages, much nicer than ours. Before going our separate ways, we agreed to meet at dawn to walk down the nearby runway to see what birds might be present in a small pond that they had heard about.

When Johnathan and I returned to our room, we discovered a dozen or more cockroaches on the walls and even on our bags. "This is horrible," I said. "Maybe we can ask for a different room, even another one being remodeled, and move."

"I doubt they have another room, since we got this room as a last resort. Maybe we should ask to move tomorrow if one of the newer rooms becomes available."

"Let's at least go to the office and check. If a better room is not available for tonight, we can make arrangements for another room for tomorrow night." Although a better room was unavailable for that night, we made arrangements to move to another room the following day.

At dawn the next day, we met the women outside their cottage and began our bird-walk down the runway. The runway was situated between the Jaguar Inn complex where we were staying and a small Mayan village on the opposite side. Although we did not see any of the residents, we did see evidence of their nightly activities. We had to walk carefully down the runway to avoid the numerous piles of defecation. And later, when returning to our rooms, we found that a dozen or more black vultures were scavenging the defecations. The women practically gagged at the sight, but I could not but think how appropriate the relationship was between the Mayans and the vultures.

"That is a perfect example of mutualism, when both the Mayans and the vultures benefit," I said.

Carol immediately responded: "You are right. What better example is there of both species benefitting? A major principal in ecology."

The four of us spent the entire day together, first birding along runway and later among the ruins and adjacent forest. It was a great day bird-wise. We recorded a total of 111 species that first day. One of the very first sightings, as we began our walk down the runway, was a pair of great curassows that flew across the runaway. Both the all-black male and the brown female had a raised crest that we saw though our binoculars when they landed on the edge of the runway and before running into the undergrowth.

"Wow!" We all four shouted at the same time. "What amazing birds," Carol said. "And that is only the start of a birding day at Tikal."

Some of the other significant sightings that morning, before spending the afternoon among the ruins, included two Yucatan poorwills, Montezuma oropendolas, many red-lored parrots, and a bat falcon. At the pond at the end of the runway, we found two gray-necked wood-rails.

The Tikal ruins, according to the brochure we had purchased at the Jaguar Inn office, stated that Tikal was the largest Mayan city in all of Mesoamerica during the 'classic period.' By 600 A.D., it was considered the Mayan capital, both politically and economically.

Johnathan said, "The brochure states that Tikal once had a population of as many as 100,000 people. And listen to this. They had a sports stadium, a hospital and a library."

Katherine asked, "Did they actually have a real library with lots of books?"

"Yes. According to the brochure, the library contained thousands of books, but today only four Mayan books still exist. I imagine that the Mayan library was lost along with the demise of the Mayan people."

"It is sad that the world has lost so much of its early human history. I would love to be able to read some of those books; they must have contained a wealth of history and details about their life."

As we wandered through the compound, I was greatly impressed with the abundant pyramids and platforms. When we reached Temple 1V, also known as the Temple of the Two Headed Snake, we stood there looking upward at the tall structure. Suddenly, a falcon flew from the top, sailed overhead, and flew on to another temple-top. I immediately cried, "Look, that is an orange-breasted falcon, one of my most-wanted birds. Check its dark back, rusty underparts and white collar. An incredible bird!"

We walked closer to where it had landed and were able to get a superb look at it through binoculars; it truly was a very special raptor. Later in the day, we all agreed that seeing that orange-breasted falcon was the highlight bird of the day.

We decided to climb to the top of Temple 1V. Up we went, finding that the way was very steep and not as easy as I had thought. By the time we reached the top, we all needed to sit and rest. But what a view it was!

Johnathan remarked, "I think we can see most of the Yucatan Peninsula from here."

Carol said, "What is most impressive to me is the size of the forest with the dozens of temples poking above the green canopy. That alone is worth the climb." We all agreed.

Suddenly we were watching a flock of birds flying over Temple 1V and not too far above our heads. I was surprised to see so many different species together. "What kind of swallows are they?" Carol asked.

"Most are rough-winged swallows, but there also are a couple gray-breasted martins, and notice the faster-flying birds with swept-backed wings. Those are swifts. The smaller ones are lesser swallow-tailed swifts, the mid-sized swifts are Vaux's swifts, and the much larger ones are black swifts."

Johnathan added: "That is the first time that I have ever seen three species of swifts together. That is very unusual, to say the least."

Two of the black swifts suddenly dived from on high and, passing near the top of the pyramid where we were sitting, we could actually feel air movement they were so close. Almost simultaneous, they sounded off with loud chipping sounds. Seconds later, the black swifts were nowhere in sight.

We began our descent from the top of Pyramid 1V. The steps were harder to negotiate going down than they had when we ascended. So, Johnathan and I helped the women. Carol had apparently taken an interest in me, as she had sat next to me at the summit, and she had directed all her questions to me; Johnathan later said that he agreed with that and that Katherine had paid greater attention to him.

Once we reached the ground and continued our tour of the ruins, Carol grabbed my hand, and we wandered around hand in hand. I noticed that Johnathan and Katherine were also paired up.

We continued to wander around the compound. Johnathan continued reading from the brochure. "It says that Tikal was originally established as a farming community; I never would have guessed that. It looks to me that the soils are primarily limestone."

"Certainly, all of the structures were built of limestone bricks," I said. "I am impressed with the height and steepness of several of the temples. More so than any others we have seen on our trip."

Johnathan said, "The brochure says that the Tikal Temple is 154 feet in height, and Temple 33 is 108 feet tall." We soon were standing in front of Temple 33. "This temple was constructed in 457 A.D. and contains the tomb of King Siya Chan K'awtil." Johnathan added, "The brochure also states that the tomb contained a single stela, which provided considerable information about Tikal to the archeologists."

After a few minutes he added, "Listen to this. According to the brochure, Temple 1V was used for sacrifices. And those sacrifices were undertaken by bow and arrow or by being disemboweled."

"What savage people those Mayans were," Carol said, "No wonder their society collapsed."

"Indeed. It suffered a slow decline after 200 A.D., and had totally collapsed by 900 A.D. However, the brochure also points out that collapse was partially due to drought and deforestation."

"Speaking of forest, it's time we began to investigate the forest to see what birds might be present," I said.

We soon entered the forest and began to identify birds. And what amazing birds we found! Some of the more attractive birds included blue-crowned motmots, barred antshrikes, pale-billed woodpeckers; blue-headed, slaty-tailed and violaceous trogons; and white-necked puffbird.

Some of smaller forest birds recorded that day included blue ground-doves, eye-ringed flatbill, spot-breasted wren, white-breasted wood-wren, cinnamon becard, red-throated ant-tanager, masked tanager, lesser and tawny-crowned greenlets, and spadebill. Spot-breasted wrens were abundant; everywhere we went, we either saw or heard these little wrens. They were easily identified by their rusty back and pale underparts with dozens of tiny black spots. Their songs consisted of a varied and rollicking series of "swee hu-a wee-a-hew" notes.

When Johnathan found and identified a spadebill, he said. "Look at that little bird ahead of us at mid-height in the vegetation; that is a spadebill. Look at its fascinating bill." We all had super looks with our binoculars. We watched the spadebill with its strange bill, creeping about within the greenery.

A few minutes later, we seemed to be in the center of a huge flock of birds that was moving about capturing insects and paying no attention to us observers. We estimated that there was at least two dozen species and as many as 150 individuals in that bird party. I was most excited at seeing a few that I had listed as target birds: several plain zenops that we watched fairly close-up, a couple black-throated and red-crowned ant-tanagers, yellow-throated euphonias, a plain ant-vireo, a dot-winged antwren, and three woodcreepers; ruddy, streak-bellied and tawny-crowned.

We had a crazy time, calling back and forth as we saw new species. Just when I was watching one species, either Johnathan or one of the women called out some other species, so I left the one I was watching and moved to the next.

Just about when I thought we had identified all the birds in that flock, Carol called, "Come look! There at about 30 feet up in vegetation is a male red-capped manakin."

We all spent several minutes watching that male and at least three others. The male manakin was going through an amazing display, making abrupt jumps and short flights, all part of its courtship behavior for the lady manakins that sat to the side of the lek watching. We watched two additional courting males, jumping about from branch to branch, snapping their wings and calling out in high, thin, drawn-out lispy calls. It was an unbelievable experience.

None of us wanted to leave this very rich habitat, but we gradually drifted out of the forest and again began to wander through the compound. Even there we found several birds that took our attention away from the ruins. I heard two separate ferruginous pygmy-owls singing their very distinct descending calls along the edge of the compound. A lone male blue bunting was searching for seeds among a patch of grass. Several golden-fronted woodpeckers and a lone black-cheeked woodpecker were feeding on a nearby tree. A pair of keel-billed toucans were sitting in another tree, apparently taking in the scene below. One tree contained four masked tityras. And there along the edge of one platform was a scaled pigeon, and dozens of parrots and parakeets passed overhead.

All the way back to our cottages, we continued to call out new birds, and each time we stopped to look. By the time we got back to the Jaguar Inn, it was early evening. We agreed to meet in the dining area in a couple hours, and Johnathan and I went to the office to find out what arrangements had been made for a new room. The manager, Manual Colón, told us that it all had been taken care of; they had even moved all our possessions into one of the new cottages. We were handed keys and told to have a good evening. We thanked Senor Colón for the move and walked over to our new quarters.

It took us another hour to shower and change before we walked over to the dining room, where we were to meet the women. It took them considerably longer than we had anticipated, so we drank a beer and talked about the extraordinary luck we had that day. When the women appeared, it was obvious that they, too, had changed for the evening.

Our conversation over dinner, once we got beyond short discussions about some of the key birds seen that day, was much more personal. Carol began talking just to me about my life while Katherine talked about similar things with Johnathan. Carol asked if I had a girlfriend back home, why I wasn't married, and if I planned to. I asked her some of the same questions, and before long we were talking about even more personal things. She admitted that she had never slept with a man, but that she wanted to. With those kinds of comments, which I welcomed, I soon asked her if she would sleep with me tonight. Her answer was, "I would like very much to sleep with you, and I think Katherine wants to spend the night with Johnathan."

After dinner we split up, Carol coming with me and Johnathan going with Katherine to their cottage. Once Carol and I were alone we began kissing, and before long our kissing became longer and more serious, and we started exploring one another. I discovered that Carol had lovely breasts. I began kissing her breasts, then her neck, and after several minutes, we undressed each other, and got in bed. The sex was marvelous, and afterword we lay together talking about odds-and-ends for a considerable time. We again made love, and before long I had drifted off to sleep. We woke up before daybreak, and we again made love while the dawn bird chorus sounded all around us.

At breakfast, the four of us talked about the day ahead. The initial plan was for Johnathan and me to taxi back to Francisco Escarcega, where we had a rental car. Carol and Katherine had rented a car and had driven to Tikal. They invited us to travel with them, which was an offer that we accepted immediately. When they said that they planned to drive to Palenque, with stops at Bonampak and Yaxchilan along the way, and if we were interested, we could all go together, that offer was accepted even faster.

Johnathan and I did realize that we had left our rental car at the airport in Francisco Escarcega. After a brief conversation, we agreed to go on to Palenque with our friends. We would visit the nearest car rental office and make arrangements for the rental car to be picked up at the Francisco Escarcega airport.

CHAPTER 9

BONAMPAK AND YAXCHILAN

OUR ROUTE FROM Tikal to Bonampak was a circuitous one; instead of driving north, we drove south to El Remate, then southwest to El Subin and west to La Tecníca, the gateway to Bonampak. Although most of the roads were open and in fair condition, several stretches were slow. The route did provide a number of opportunities to stop and walk into the forest. By the time we reached El Subin, located along the Rio El Subin, it was lunchtime. Instead of eating in a restaurant, we bought some rolls and cheese at a little store, and ate on the riverbank.

It was a gorgeous day, not too hot and with a mild breeze that kept flies to a minimum. The Rio El Sabin was lined with cypress trees, a few willows, and a huge sycamore. Patches of wildflowers were scattered here and there on the riverbank.

Carol was first to admire the setting, and before she finished her comment, she exclaimed, "Look, there is a kingfisher! I think it is an Amazon kingfisher. I have never seen one before." Sure enough, we all were looking at that kingfisher, that was sitting on a low branch just across the river. Within seconds, Carol added, "My gosh, just above the kingfisher is a turquoise-browed motmot. Look at its long tail." The bird remained in place, so we had a long look at it. It wagged its tail back and forth and called out a rhythmic "k'wok k'wok" call.

As we sat on the riverbank, we continued to search the vegetation for other species, and we were not disappointed. During the approximately two hours we spent for lunch, we recorded two dozen or more birds. Other than several brightly colored tanagers, the bird of the day was a male resplendent quetzal that flew into the sycamore tree. We were awed by that bird with its bright-green and red plumage and extremely long streamer tail. "I suspect that our quetzal may have a nest in that tree, I said. "They nest in cavities, and you can bet that big old sycamore has cavities." Although we kept watching the tree, a female quetzal did not appear, nor did we see a cavity that might contain a nest.

After a while, the women decided to walk along the river, and Johnathan and I walked the other direction. In about twenty minutes, we returned to our picnic spot, and Carol announced that, just down the river a short distance, was a muddy area below the bank where there were "at least a hundred butterflies puddling." She described a few, although none of us knew butterflies, so we decided to walk down to the puddling site. When we got there, we found that there were hundreds of butterflies of all colors. The majority were yellow, but many were orange and brown, and many were multicolored. There were butterflies of all sizes, from tiny blues to large swallowtails. As we stood there admiring the throng on the muddy puddle, a huge iridescent blue butterfly flew pass along the river. I said, "You know, I have seen butterflies all my life, but I never really looked at them. After this experience, I am going to learn butterflies."

We soon were on our way to Bonampak, but because we had spent so much of the day along the Rio Subin, it was almost dark when we arrived at La Técnica. By the time we found a hotel and settled in, Johnathan and Katherine in one room and Carol and I in another, we all were ready for dinner. The La Cocíno was close enough to walk to, so we chose that restaurant, and were soon eating. Although our meals were not outstanding, there was plenty of food. We returned to our rooms after walking about town, and sitting at the plaza for a while. I already was looking forward to spending another night with Carol.

Once we were alone, we soon were in bed and enjoying each other's eager bodies. That night's love-making was even more enjoyable than the night before. I honestly wondered if maybe I was falling in love. Since I had never felt the way I was feeling about Carol, I decided to just enjoy our time together and let destiny take its course.

The next morning, after breakfast, we drove across the Usumacinta River, which serves as the border between Guatemala and Mexico, and into the state of Chiapas and the ruins of Bonampak. After paying our entrance fees and buying a brochure, we entered the compound. The first structure we saw was a platform with a temple built on top. "That is 'Structure One,' according to the brochure," Johnathan said. It had been built into a hillside and we could see, even from a distance, that the temple walls were covered with murals. We immediately walked over to get a better look.

"These murals relate to what must have been the Bonampak culture; they all tell about war and sacrificing their enemies and probably their own people for whatever reasons their leaders divined," Katherine said.

"I'll tell you one thing," I said. "These murals debunk any thoughts that these Mayans were a peaceful people."

"This structure was built in the 8th century. Although the murals are extremely faded, according to the brochure, they once were rich colors of Maya blue, blue-green, red and yellow."

"Look on that wall, there is a band of glyphs," Johnathan said. He added, "There is a total of 80 glyphs in a band that wraps around the building."

As we looked over the building, we could see that, above each room, were niches in the walls that contained seated figures. One niche contained figures depicting a man being sacrificed, and other niches showed even more warriors sacrificing victims.

"According to the brochure," Johnathan said, "Many of the murals were done under the leadership of Yajaw Chaan Muwan and were designed to depict a great battle on January 12, 787."

He added, "Bonampak was considered only a minor power, and during the years of its existence, from 500 to 800, it was subject to Yaxchilán. But Bonampak died out soon after 800, probably due to overpopulation and deforestation. It started as a farming community, as early as 250 B.C., but militarized soon afterwards, and was defeated by Yaxchilán in 400 A.D."

After a few minutes, Johnathan added: "The brochure also states that the site is still held in esteem by many of the older Mayans who come to Bonampak to worship at least annually."

Although we were not paying a great attention to the birds while we were walking about the ruins, we did walk into the adjacent forest to see what might be there. We had barely stepped into the forest when a squirrel cuckoo attracted our attention when it flew to the open branches, where we had an excellent view. We looked at that long reddish bird for several minute; it seemed to be poising for us. "That is one amazing first-bird in this forest," Katherine said.

Although we spent only about an hour in the Bonampak forest, the list we tallied that evening at dinner included such target birds as chestnut-colored woodpecker, slate-headed tody-flycatcher, buff-throated forest gleaner, long-billed gnatwren, crimson-headed tanager, and green honeycreeper. When we came out of the forest, we came upon a small field covered with wildflowers.

Carol was first to notice that site, and we watching several hummingbirds feeding on the colorful blossoms. Two of those hummers were on my target list: black-crested coquette and white-tailed emerald. Just as we were about to move elsewhere, a bananaquit appeared. "Look, a bananaquit," I said. "That bird is the official bird of St. Croix, and seeing it here on the Yucatan is really special. But it almost makes me homesick."

It is strange, how when one is busy with new birds, new places, and new friends, one's home and family are seldom remembered. I said, "Please remind me to write a letter to my parents tonight. I seem to have forgotten how important they are to me."

Carol walked over to me and gave me a big hug. We walked away from the hummingbird field hand in hand. Although there was still more to see at Bonampak, we were getting restless and decided that, since we learned that the more dominant city during that period was Yaxchilan, very close to Bonampak, we decided that we also should visit that site. Johnathan said, "You know, I have known about Bonampak for years, but I have never known about Yaxchilan. Now I find out that Yaxchilan is a more important city than Bonampak."

Carol said, "That is true for me too, but I know why it has come to my attention. Several of my birding friends have spent time in the Lacadona forest area, usually after birding in Palenque, and they have mentioned going to San Cristobal and the Lacadona forest, but never once mentioned Yaxchilan. I remember that they told me that is where golden-cheeked warblers are often found in winter."

"Yes," I said, "I have seen golden-cheeks in in the Texas hill country, and I remember our birding guide, Victor Emanuel, telling us that they over-winter near San Cristobal."

Because it was only early afternoon, we decided to return to La Técnica and visit Yaxchilan that was right on the western edge of La Técnica. We stopped briefly at our rooms as we passed through town, and within another half-hour, we were walking around the Yaxchilan compound.

According to the brochure that we purchased at the entrance, Yaxchilan was the most powerful military city on the Yucatan. Although Yaxchilan did not have the murals or the tall temples as did Bonampak and Tikal, it was a much larger complex, although only a few of the structures had been excavated.

"Its early history started with enthronement events of Yopoat B'alam on July 23, 359, according to the brochure," Johnathan said. He added that the city contains a total 67 structures that have been identified as well as 50 lintels and 35 stelae.

"We have already seen various stelae in other ruins, but I'm not sure if we have seen lintels," I said. By then we were standing in front of Structure 33. "I guess I am looking at lintels just above the doorway of this structure. They look pretty well preserved, too. I also am looking at well-preserved stelae that are standing in front of the building. That one to the right contains some hieroglyphs that, if I could read them, I would probably tell you all about the history of Yaxchilan."

"That is exactly what the brochures states that they contain the entire dynamic history of the city and its relationship to other cities," Johnathan said. "Apparently, Yaxchilan was in a continuous war-like relations with both Bonampak and Piedras Negras."

Structure 19 was identified as a labyrinth, and the marker stated that it is a temple with rooms spread over three levels that are linked by interior stairways.

"That seems fairly sophisticated; I wonder who lived there," Carol said. "Maybe one of the king's maidens; you do know that those early Mayans had lots of wives."

"And," Johnathan added, "if any of the wives didn't treat the king with total respect at all times, they were handed over to the guy in charge of sacrifices."

"I know you made that up, but after all, the abundant inscriptions that are scattered all over the place needed something to feature.

Suddenly, high overhead, was a huge bird. It took me a few seconds to realize that it was a king vulture. "King vulture," I shouted, and instantly we all were watching that amazing bird through our binoculars.

It had found a thermal and was floating in huge circles. I saw that there were a number of soaring birds alongside the vulture. Besides the king vulture, there were several turkey vultures, a couple of yellow-headed vultures, lone black-collared and white hawks, and a great black hawk. It took me several minutes to identify it for sure because of its similarity to the common black hawk.

"Look off to the left, I think that smaller raptor is a short-tailed hawk," Johnathan said.

"I thing you are right. Good call!" I said. Soaring with the first bunch of birds was a black-and-white hawk-eagle. "That is incredible! Would you believe that?"

We must have stood there for a half-hour or more just watching the kettle of hawks and vultures. Finally, Carol said, "It is because of times like this that I became a birder. And, I bet that if we spend more time in the forest we would find several more lifer raptors."

With that, we resumed our wanderings through the ruins, although we constantly watched the sky for more raptors. We did not see any more soaring birds but we found several birds along the river. Muscovy ducks were fairly common and, in one place with emergent vegetation there were three masked ducks and a boat-billed heron. We stopped there, and I began squeaking to see what other birds could be attracted. The sound attracted a bare-throated tiger-heron which arose from the tules, flew a dozen feet, and plopped down again. I continued squeaking, and a pinnated bittern suddenly appeared and flew down river, but we all got a really good look at the bird that was lifer for all four of us.

We eventually returned to the Yaxchilan compound, where we found a ballcourt right off of the Main Plaza. Stela at Structure 35 depicts Lady Evenstar, the mother of Bird Jaguar IV. And stela 33 was sculptured from a stalactite. "I know that the majority of the Yucatan is limestone, and caves are commonplace, but I wonder where they acquired this stalactite," Johnathan said.

We saw less than half of all the structures that were available at Yaxchilan before we were ready to head back across the river to our rooms in La Técnica. Just before we reached our car, Johnathan yelled, "Look ahead of us in that tall tree. There is a laughing falcon perched on a bare branch near the very top." Once again, we stopped before we got too close and gazed at that raptor. We were close enough, however, so we could readily see its white head with a black mask, a chocolate brown back, and banded tail.

"What a bird to close our day!" Carol said.

CHAPTER 10

PALENQUE

WE SPENT ANOTHER night in La Técina. At breakfast in the morning, we talked about the Bonampak and Yaxchilan ruins and the marvelous birds we had seen. We agreed that the Bonampak murals were the highlight of the ruins, but we couldn't agree on which of the abundant birds was the favorite. For me, the king vulture was most memorable, Johnathan chose the black-and-white hawk-eagle, and Carol and Katherine chose the quetzal, but we all agreed that many of the birds we had seen were special.

Our conversation soon turned to our next destination - Palenque. It was a fairly easy drive, straight up Highway 307 about 50 miles to the city of Palenque and the ruins. We still had the car the women had rented and, when I asked about their plans to return it, Katherine said, "When we rented the car, we arranged to return it turn it at Palenque, so we're good to go."

As soon as we got to Palenque, we rented two rooms at Cabanes Kin Balam Palenque, right at the entrance to the Palenque compound. The rooms were clean, and a restaurant was available on site. Realizing that, once we entered the Palenque compound, we would probably would not want to leave for something to eat, we ate at the La Reyna Roja. Our lunch was adequate, but we were anxious to get into the ruins.

Johnathan's guidebook included Palenque, so we did not need to purchase a brochure at the entrance; we paid our entrance fee, which was good for up to three days, and we entered the compound.

"I can't believe I am really here," Johnathan said. "I have dreamed about Palenque most of my life. My father has told me about Palenque ever since I was a little boy. I only wish he could be with us now."

"My parents probably never heard of Palenque, although they constantly encourage me to travel and see as much of the world as possible before I married and settled down," I said. "My mother believes that once a man married, it was his responsibility to produce grandchildren that she could spoil."

"Well, Robert, I am glad that you refrained from marrying at least until after this trip," Johnathan said. "I know that you will always be glad that you waited. Do you have a girlfriend back home that you might marry?"

"No, I do not," I said. "I guess that I have not yet met the girl of my dreams. In fact, I have never had a serious relationship. St. Croix does not offer a very good selection. How about you?"

"Miami has lots of women, and I did meet someone two years ago that I thought might be the one, but that was not to be. Just about the time that I was thinking about marriage, she announced that she was going to marry one of my friends."

I turned to the women and asked, "How about you two? Any close calls?"

Carol and Katherine shook their heads, and Katherine said, "I got very close my first year in college, and just when I thought maybe, I found my friend in bed with one of my girlfriends. And that was the end of that relationship."

Johnathan began to read from the guidebook. "Palenque means 'fortified place' in Mayan, although its original name was Lakamhe. It contained more than 1000 structures. It was first settled about 300 B.C., but did not reach its peak for another six hundred years. Then, until the end of the seventh century, it was the Mayan pacesetter as a religious and political center. This was the 'classic period' for Palenque when the pyramids, aqueduct, and numerous other structures were built, many of which represent the finest known examples of Mayan culture. This period of growth and development probably reached a peak about 700 A.D, and then gradually declined until the site was deserted in the late ninth century."

"But why was it deserted," Carol asked. "And how many people lived there and where did they go?"

"The reason for the abandonment is not entirely clear, although most archeologists speculate that it was directly related to the collapse of Palenque's agricultural system." In another minute, he added, "At the same time, there was a general revolt against the harsh rule of the priestly caste that acted to destroy the social structure and government. As for the number of inhabitants, I haven't found that number yet, but I have found where it was the most populated than any Mayan city."

We continued to walk about the ruins, and soon we were standing in front of the Temple of Inscriptions.

"Johnathan, tell us about this structure. It must have its own story," I said.

"Yes, indeed. According to the guidebook, it wasn't until 1952 that archeologists discovered an inner chamber containing the tomb of a priest or ruler called Pacal the Great, who ruled from 615 to 683. It was the first sarcophagus ever found in a Mayan pyramid. The chamber also included a huge variety of precious stones, a red-painted tooth and bones, as well as fragments of a jade mask. I think we can see a reproduction of that mask in the museum.

"According to the guidebook, finding a sarcophagus changed all earlier theories that the Mayan pyramids were little more than the base for temples that were constructed on top, not built as burial sites. The crypt contained six standing and three seated stucco priests, larger than life-size, on guard."

"That is amazing. Does the guidebook tell about size of the crypt?" Carol asked.

Johnathan read some more, "The sarcophagus was ten feet long and seven feet wide and with a five-ton lid that was covered with numerous hieroglyphs. Here's more. The tomb contained another feature that had not previously been discovered in Mexico, a small tube leading from the tomb up through the entire structure to very near the floor of the temple building. Many archeologists believe that the tube, called a 'psychoduct,' was like the *sipapu* of Hopi kivas, to allow communcations between the priests and the underground spirits."

I could not help but marvel about such things, and said, "Johnathan, I have read about the Hopi culture, and hearing about similarities between

Mayan and Hopis is fascinating. I wonder if it is possible that those early Mayans, after they left Palenque, could possibly have wandered to the American Southwest? I wonder if there are other similarities."

"That could certainly be a study that some student could use for a graduate degree. It would make a great thesis. I am told that there are some linguistic similarities. I wonder if any ambitious archeological student might already be working on such a thesis."

We talked about that idea for several minutes as we wandered about the compound, and later, after leaving Palenque, we brought the idea up again. I said, "If I were to attend a university, I would love to study archeology; I already have a thesis."

"But Robert, I thought you had already decided to study ornithology. Maybe you could study avian similarities within the Southwest and Mayan lands." We all got a chuckle about that idea.

Our next stop within the Palenque compound was at The Palace, the structure that is considered the most complex of Palenque's numerous structures. The Palace contains twenty-five rooms resting on an artificial platform that is 228 feet long and 180 feet wide. Johnathan read in the guidebook that "several of the lower rooms were used for steam baths, complete with drains in the floors which led to underground aqueducts. Other rooms were used for bathrooms that were connected to a separate septic tank." In a few minutes, he added: "The Palace also contained a tower marked by the astronomical symbol of Venus on the third level, suggesting that this could have been an astrological observatory.

"A separate septic system suggests that those early peoples were much more attuned to healthy conditions than many of their ancestors. I am thinking, of course, of the Mayans that lived along the runway at Tikal."

Just behind the fascinating ruins is an equally fascinating world of tropical rain-forest, complete with all of the unique flora and fauna that occur in those natural settings. We decided to postpone our forest adventure until the following day because it already was late in the day. We walked back to our rooms, stopped there briefly, and drove into town, where we parked and found a restaurant that looked clean and welcoming. Afterwards, we spent a couple of hours walking around town, admiring some of the old buildings. The ancient cathedral was most impressive.

Dawn found us back at Palenque and we soon were wandering along the outer edge of the forest that abutted the compound. A few of the birds we found almost immediately included a keel-billed toucan, chestnut-headed and Montezuma oropendolas, chestnut-collared aracari, yellow-bellied elaenia, scrub and olive-backed euphonias, masked tanager, and yellow-tailed oriole.

We entered the forest interior, and it was alive with birds of all colors and shapes. Three species that commanded our attention were a blue-crowned motmot and both citreoline and violaceous trogons. Wherever we looked were birds. It was a great start to our first full day in the Palenque forest.

Unexpectedly we encountered three other birders, two sisters, Katrina and Margaret, and their brother, Hans. We introduced ourselves and began comparing information about some of the birds that we had seen with species they had found.

Hans asked, "Have you found an Aplomado falcon yet?"

"No," I said. "But that is one of the birds that we hoped to see. Have you found one, and if so where."

The three grinned at each other, and Katrina said, "We saw one last evening and I can tell you exactly where you can find it."

"Where?" Johnathan and I said at same time.

Katrina continued: "If you go into town at dusk and sit in front of the cathedral, an Aplomado will fly down the street toward the cathedral, circle over the front steps and continue back down the street, picking off insects from the street lights. We learned about this location from another birding group, and we have seen the bird there the last two evenings."

That evening after an early dinner, where we again met our three friends, we all walked from the restaurant to the cathedral and sat on the front steps in anticipation of an Aplomado. And just when the street lights were turned on, we found our Aplomado flying toward us catching cicadas at each light. It flew directly over us and then circled back and continued to feed at each light as it headed back down the street and disappeared into the darkening sky.

"Well," I said. "That was one of the easiest lifers I can remember." we congratulated one another and then stopped off at out little restaurant to celebrate with a cold cerveza.

We returned to the forest the next morning and walked along one of the trails in search of more birds. And what a morning it was! We found an enormous number of species, especially within the thicker areas of the forest. Perhaps the bird of the day was a male great antshrike, a large (eight inches) black-and-white, crested bird with striking red eyes. It had been perched very close to me, but I did not see it until it flew away and across an army-ant mass that was crossing the trail. It stopped just long enough to capture a huge green insect of some kind, tear it apart with its shrike-like bill, and swallow the three or four pieces. It then flew off to where it disappeared into the foliage.

"That was one terrific bird," Johnathan said. "But let's take a look at this mass of army ants. Are you aware that some tropical birds actually follow army ants to feed on the various insects and other tiny creatures they disturb as they move from place to place?

"I have read about army ants, but I have never experienced them in the wild." So, we spent the next hour or so watching them as they walked across trees and into holes and burrows. The mass moved reasonably slowly so that many of the more mobile species in their path were able to escape. However, when they escaped the ants, they exposed themselves to other predators that took advantage of their predicament.

We noticed that the mass of ants had attracted a number of birds, which were capturing many of the insects that were fleeing from the ants. I knew that there is a group of tropical birds called "antbirds," and we saw several that day in the Palenque forest. Early on, I had heard the distinct calls of common and red-crowned ant-tanagers, and we watched both of those birds, as well as several more species, all following the army ants.

A strange chattering call attracted me to a black-throated shrike-tanager. It had just captured a large green katydid, which it swallowed whole. Just behind it, dashing here and there among the tangle of vines, was a tiny black bird with one white wing bar below a series of tiny white dots. Although I had never seen it before, I immediately was able to identify it as a dot-winged antwren.

And that's the way it went, identifying bird after bird, until the army ants moved away into a deep ravine and out of sight. It was a memorable time, and we talked about that experience many times later.

That evening during dinner, we made a list of the birds found that day. Some of the additional species seen at the army-ant colony included squirrel cuckoo, blue-crowned motmot, royal, sulphur-rumped and ochre-bellied flycatchers; white-breasted wood-wren, and several warblers, including a number of North American species and two Mexico-only species, golden-browed and fan-tailed warblers.

Army-ants are some of the most interesting creatures of the tropical forests. Their presence affects every other living thing. The colony follows a nomadic life-style, moving about only during the daytime, from one overnight bivouac site to another. These sites may include a variety of protected places, from hollow logs to overhangs. An army of ants may number up to twenty million individuals, and a mass of little black ants, moving about one foot per minute, represents a formidable influence upon the environment.

Although we understood the basics of army ants, we did not fully appreciate them until after I read more about them. To paraphrase what I read, here is a general summary:

> Every morning the army leaves the bivouac site, led by the largest soldiers, in search of food. Captured prey is passed back along the column for use by the smallest worker and large winged males that service the lone queen. The largest soldiers, often three times the size of the smaller workers, are concentrated along the outer edge of the colony. These soldier ants possess extremely heavy, sickle-shaped jaws. Amazon Indians use these large-jawed ants for "stitching" wounds. Once the ants are enticed to bite across a wound, which holds the edges together, the rest of the ant's body is twisted away to leave the head serving as a natural clamp.
>
> The army-ant colony captures or consumes almost every edible creature in its path. The mass movement, which can form a hundred-foot-wide front, can create considerable havoc among the wildlife that it encounters.

We had another fascinating sighting after leaving the army ants while returning to our rooms. Very near the outer edge of the forest, we passed a large thicket, where we heard odd sounds, like someone snapping their fingers, that were coming from the thicket. It took us several minutes to find what was making that sound, and when we did, we saw a little short-tailed bird. Johnathan excitedly exclaimed, "It's a white-tailed manakin!" It was a new trip bird for all of us, although I had read about its wing-snapping behavior. Emmet Blake's, *Birds of Mexico*, had described its dance thusly: "The male jumps back and forth between two twigs, the dancer usually landing facing its previous perch, and each jump initiated by a loud 'snap' of the wings."

During the time we spent in the forest, we could hear the loud, booming calls of howler monkeys, but we had not had a really good look at one of these arboreal creatures. However, just after watching the army-ants we noticed a number of howlers in the high canopy, watching us. Although they were quiet at first, once they realized that we had found them, they no longer were silent but began to bombard us with howls.

"There must be a dozen or more," Carol said. "And look over there to the right. I see at least four females carrying babies on their back. There must be at least fifteen to twenty individuals."

Although the troop was moving away from us, we had a good ten or more minutes of observations before they disappeared into the forest. Even then, we heard them howling away.

Johnathan said, "I guess we should be thankful that they did not pelt us with excrement. I have heard that they do that when aroused."

"I think that is an old wives' tale, and not really true for howlers, I said. "It is true I am told, for some of the African species."

"I think it is more because we are such upstanding citizens," he responded.

"The guidebook states that howlers are the largest New World monkeys, and that they normally occur in groups of six to fifteen individuals. That would fit with our sighting. It also states that a typical family consists of one to three adult males and multiple females."

"From what we saw of our troop, with young, that would also be about right." I asked, "Does the guidebook explain how howlers are able to howl so loudly?"

"Yes, it states that howlers produce their loud, deep guttural howls due to an enlarged hyoid bone. It also states that they call most often at dusk and dawn, and their howls can be heard for three miles."

"Here's something more," he said. "The early Mayans considered howler monkeys to be divine. Some groups believed that they were gods."

"I must admit that encountering howlers at Palenque added a certain melodrama to our Palenque experience, but in no way are they divine."

CHAPTER 11

VILLAHERMOSA AND CATEMACO

THE FOLLOWING MORNING, after our day at Palenque that had ended with howler monkeys, we sat at breakfast for longer than normal to make some decisions about our next few days. The women had already told us that they must leave Mexico and return to Berkeley. Although both had graduated, they had yet to complete their thesis. Johnathan and I realized that we would miss them, but we also understood how important their educations were.

After a lengthy discussion, we decided to head for Villahermosa, where they would be able to connect with a flight to San Francisco, and we would continue to Catemaco. Johnathan suggested they check with the local travel agency about flight times, so that we would have a better idea about scheduling our day. Soon after breakfast, they asked the woman who ran the travel office at our hotel about flights from Villahermosa. We learned that only early-morning flights were available to California. That left us with most of the day free to do what we wanted. The women did make reservations for the next day's flight from Villahermosa to San Francisco.

Our conversation continued about whether we should go back into the Palenque forest or head for Villahermosa. Our decision was an easy one; we would spend the rest of the morning at Palenque and drive to Villahermosa in the afternoon, get rooms for the night, and be able to deliver the women to the airport in the morning.

Another morning in the Palenque forest was just as exciting as it had been the two previous mornings. We found a different trail behind the ruins that we had not noticed before. We slowly walked along watching birds and enjoying each and every one. There was something very special about finding species that we had not seen earlier. I couldn't help but comment, "You can bet that if we were able spend several more days here, every day we would see new species. This forest would continue to produce more and more species." Just as I said that, a loud, explosive whistle call, like "p-wee-e-loo!" emanated from the high canopy just ahead. I immediately knew that it was a rufous piha, but it took us several minutes to locate it. When we did, we were a little disappointed. It was an all- rusty-colored bird with a black bill and whitish eyerings. But its most notable feature was its loud explosive call, and that was not at all disappointing.

Other forest birds we found that morning included three hummingbirds that we had not found previously: white-bellied emerald, long-billed starthroat, and purple-crowned fairy. Later, when we left the forest to return to our rooms, a flock of white-crowned parrots flew overhead. That evening at dinner, when we tallied all the birds seen at Palenque, our list numbered 165 species.

Our trip to Villahermosa was without incident. We passed the airport before entering the city and, by late afternoon, we had found a nearby motel and had settled in. When we asked about a nearby restaurant, the Casa Rodrígues, just down the block, was recommended. Before heading out for dinner, Carol and I decided to shower first, and that evolved into a passionate love-making. Maybe because we would soon part, our affection for one another seemed to reach a climax. And by the time we met up with Johnathan and Katherine, it seemed that they too had enjoyed a special time together.

Dinner that evening was excellent, but none of us seemed to appreciate our food as we should have. At least for me, in spite of looking forward to our continuing adventure in Mexico, I had become extremely fond of Carol, and I wondered if I would ever find another woman that could make me happier than she. Afterwards, alone in our room, we talked about how we might continue our growing relationship. But we understood that, once she returned to her studies and I continued on in Mexico and eventually returned home to St. Croix, any further relationship would be extremely difficult. We did agree to write often and call when we could.

In the morning, we drove to the airport and walked Carol and Katherine to the boarding gate, where we stood close to each other. There was nothing more to say. I gave Carol a long hug and kiss just before she boarded. Johnathan and I watched the flight take off before we walked out of the airport to our car. We drove out to the highway and were soon en route to Catemaco.

"Johnathan," I said, "I am very close to being in love with Carol, and I even thought of asking her to marry me, but I couldn't. I suspect that we both will go our own ways and will, in the not too distant future find someone else. At the moment, however, I feel very sad."

"Robert, I have the same feeling about Katherine, but she told me this morning that she had used this trip to help her make a decision about accepting a marriage proposal from a long-time friend back home."

"Did she say she had made a decision?"

"No. She told me that she felt more confused now than before. We agreed to write to one another and to see what the future might hold. My personal opinion is that she will not agree to marry her friend, but will finish her education before making any decision one way or the other. I will be really interested in what she does. But I don't think she and I will ever be together."

The town of Catemaco is situated at about 1,200 feet elevation on the northern shore of Laguna de Catemaco, a freshwater lake about ten miles long and surrounded by the foothills of Sierra de Tuxtla. The lake is considered by many to be the most beautiful lake in Mexico. The human population of Catemaco is about 30,000, but the town serves a much larger population of farmers, fishermen, and the like that live nearby.

Arriving in Catemaco, we drove around the town for a short time, and we soon found accommodations at the Motel Plaza Azul, located along the lakeshore. We obtained a map of the area from the clerk at the motel, Carmen Fernando; she seemed to be very familiar with the region and also aware of the best locations for birds. Catemaco has long had a reputation as a favorite site for Christmas Bird Counts; several birders from the states make annual pilgrimages to Catemaco to participate. Carmen told us about six key sites used during the Christmas counts. She wrote them down: 1. the Los Tuxtlas biological field station and surroundings south of town, 2. a trail that goes up into the forest from the station, 3. the road beyond the station that ends at the coast and the village of Montepio, 4. the lake shore roadway that goes totally around the lake, and 5. the highlands of the San Martín that is accessible from the roadway that branches off the lake shore drive, and 6. the area of Catemaco itself.

Although we did not have a full afternoon by the time we got our room at the Playa Azul, we decided to drive out toward the research station for the reminder of the day; it was a good decision. The vegetation along the first part of the roadway was second-growth rain-forest, but before we reached the research station, we found mature rain-forest habitat. We got out of the car and began birding along the roadway. Right away we found a tall fig tree that contained at least a dozen birds.

"Robert, there is a lovely cotinga, to the right of center; what a beautiful bird!" It was overall bright cobalt-blue, except for patches of deep, rich purple on its throat and chest; its wings and tail are black edged with purple. I later read that its Spanish name is *asulejo real*, meaning little royal blue. "Look beyond the cotinga, there is a pair of blue-crowned clorophonias." We called out a dozen more birds, including two bright hummingbirds - azure-crowned and rufous-tailed hummingbirds - all feeding in that same bromeliad-festooned tree.

While we stood there admiring the cotinga and the chlorophonias, a double-billed kite took off from the same tree, circled us and flew off towards the lake. As the kite disappear, we saw another raptor circling nearby, a black hawk-eagle. We could hardly control our excitement. "Johnathan, with what we are finding in the first couple hours in the middle of the day, one can only imagine what we are going to find in the morning. What a rich area for birds!"

It wasn't long before the day had slipped away and we slowly drove back to Catemaco and Playa Azul, checking the birds along the way. As we passed a marshy area that we had not noticed earlier, we decided to stop and see what might be there. Barely 30 feet off the roadway, and sitting on a post, was a Muscovy duck. The sky was suddenly filled with birds. Hundreds of parrots and herons were among the flocks apparently going to nighttime roosts.

We were pleasantly surprised at the dinner that night; it was one of the better meals so far on our trip. Also, at dinner we met a small group of birders who were just completing a five-day birding visit of the region.

We introduced ourselves and were soon trading information. We had just arrived at Catemaco, and they were en route to Palenque. By the time we returned to our room, we had made several notes about where to find birds in the Catemaco area.

Before dawn the next morning, we drove out the road we had visited briefly the previous day. It was necessary to drive carefully because of the numerous pauraques we encountered perched on the roadway. We reached the Los Tuxtlas biological station at dawn, and we soon were walking up and down the nearby roadway. We found several of the same species from yesterday and added another two-dozen species that we had not seen previously. Directly across from the station was a trail that climbed into the forest. We grabbed our packs and canteens and began our hike.

Trailside birding was spectacular that day. We heard citreoline, collared, and violaceous trogon calls constantly. We watched a blue-crowned motmot, the largest of the Mexican motmots, as it sat quietly on a tree branch, moving its strange racket-shaped tail from side to side like a slow pendulum. We counted a total of 25 black-throated shrike-tanagers during the day, and I found a plain xenops, about the size of a small sparrow, that we watched hanging from the vegetation. When it passed across a sunny patch, we were surprised that its plumage changed from a subtle buffy color to a rich reddish-colored back and tail.

About a mile above the research station was a small Indian village that we skirted as best we could. Beyond the village, the trail gradually dropped down along a forested slope to a small but sparkling blue lake. The lake was one of the most surprising and welcome sights of the day. It was like a bright jewel imbedded in the green slopes of the Sierra de Tuxtla. As we got closer, we found a lone fisherman on the lake, standing in a dugout canoe. We watched him as he cast his net and when he pulled it back in, he had netted one to three pan-sized fish with each cast.

Johnathan suddenly said, "Robert, there is a white hawk soaring along the slope beyond the lake." That soaring white hawk provided a marvelous contrast with the blue lake and green rain forest. It was a memory that I will long cherish from that day.

The most common bird in the forest that day was the brown jay. There were at least 45 of these large corvids, including several yellow-billed youngsters. Almost as common was the boat-billed flycatcher. Both of these bird species could be heard constantly uttering loud obnoxious calls. We added several band-backed and spot-breasted wrens and yellow-winged tanagers to the chorus which produced a very noisy patch of forest.

All along the trail, we had encountered a number of the local folks walking up and down the hill, most with huge packs filled with almost everything imaginable. One man was carrying a pig, another three chickens, and yet another with a bundle that appeared to be produce.

Later, I said to Johnathan, "Did you notice their feet? Almost every one of those folks were barefooted, and their feet were almost as wide as long."

"I guess if we walked up and down that muddy trail as much as they do, our feet would be square, too."

The following day, we decided to drive into the Santa Marta highlands, the area on the far side of the lake. Just past the village of Coyame, we took a side-road to the east to the village Bastonal. Although the road was little more than a trail, and much of the vegetation had been cut for agriculture purposes, the occasional patches of forest did produce a few hard-to-find birds: purplish-backed quail-dove, emerald toucanet, scaly-throated foliage-gleaner, black robin, and plain-breasted brush-finch. We got excited about the emerald toucanet. "There it is, finally," I said. "This is one of the birds I had excepted to find earlier, but it has eluded us until today."

"What a colorful bird! It is smaller than the toucans. I wonder, since it does not have as wide a range as the keel-billed toucan, if it might be hunted out. I have heard that this area of Mexico provides a good many birds to ornithological collections. It would be a shame if the emerald toucanet becomes another dodo."

Although we spent much of the day in the Santa Marta highlands, we were disappointed. Too much of the landscape had been turned from forest to fields of corn and a few other crops.

The next day, we decided to drive to the research station and beyond to the end of the road. We stopped numerous times along the way and each time found an amazing variety of birds, many of which were trip birds. The road ends at the tiny fishing village of Montepio at the mouth of the Río Máquino. We spend only a couple hours there but we added a number of birds, such as gulls and terns, that we had not yet recorded. The bird of the day, which we found in the river, was a sungrebe. We spent several minutes watching that bird swimming near the far riverbank, and when we slowly walked toward it for a better look, it called a high-pitched reedy trill. We had come too close because it apparently realized that we were watching it, and it dove and disappeared. After searching for it for several minutes, we gave up, but we congratulated one another; it was one of my target birds.

The other bird of note that day was a peregrine. We found that falcon soaring along the coastline, not too far-off shore, and although we did not see it take any prey, it was an impressive bird nonetheless. I told Johnathan, "Peregrines are the world's fastest bird; they have been recorded at 140 miles per hour, and they have been recorded almost everywhere in the world. They are even found at St. Croix during the winter months."

By the time we got back to Catemaco, it was dinnertime. During our meal, Johnathan brought up the subject of ruins. "You know, Robert, the main reason for my visiting Mexico is to see ruins. And although I have been perfectly happy to bird along the way and even go out of our way to find birds, I am ready to get back to seeing more ruins."

"You are right, we have seen some super birds, but I will agree with whatever you want to do at this point."

"I suggest we head for Monte Alban near Oaxaca. Monte Alban is a classic Mayan ruin, and the city of Oaxaca is set in a valley with high mountains nearby. That area offers both ruins and new birds. What do you think about going there next?"

"That sounds like a super idea!"

However, before leaving Catemaco, I posted a long letter to my parents. Maybe because I still felt guilty for not remaining in Miami and going to college, I wanted them to understand how much I was enjoying my adventures in Mexico.

CHAPTER 12

OAXACA AND MONTE ALBAN

WE LEFT CATEMACO the next morning and headed southwest toward Juan Rodriguez, then on to Playa Vicente, where we took a smaller highway to Santiago Choapan and Totenpec. From there it was about 60 miles on Highway 175 to Oaxaca. That highway gradually climbed from the lowlands onto a mid-elevation plateau and then crossed higher mountains to where it steeply descended into the valley of Oaxaca.

I had already read considerable material about Mexico and the state of Oaxaca. I told Johnathan that the state of Oaxaca is famous for its diversity of birds. "Oaxaca has a greater number of birds of any of the Mexican states. I read one study, published in 1980, that reported a grand total of 681 species, and that's more than has been found in the entire countries of Guatemala or Honduras, countries well known for their natural resources."

"Why so many species in Mexico," Johnathan asked.

"Because Mexico has such a variety of habitats, from the coniferous forests, to cloud forest, to mid-elevation forests, lower elevation rain-forests, and woodlands such as oak-pine forests and pinyon-juniper woodlands, and many lowland woodlands. And think about the coastal areas and the abundant rivers and lakes.

"I remember reading somewhere about how the early Spanish conquistadors described Mexico. When they returned to Spain and the King asked for a description of the new land, a returning conquistador seized a piece of paper, crushed it into a crinkled ball, and then laid it in front of the King. "There, your majesty, is a map of your New Spain." The crinkled ball was a good representation of Mexico's contrasting peaks, ridge, slopes, and valleys.

Before reaching the mountains, we found a little lane off the highway that ran between tall cactuses to a field that was surrounded by arid tropical-scrub vegetation. The field contained corn stalks that were already two feet high, and a scarecrow that did not seem to frighten any of the birds. In fact, several painted buntings and blue grosbeaks were feeding at its feet.

"Let's get out and walk and see what else we might find," I said. Soon after we began to wander through the field, Johnathan suddenly shouted, "Robert, look, there is a male orange-breasted bunting, one of our target birds." It was a gorgeous bird, with plumage that was a combination of blue and yellow and a bright yellowish-green crown. A few other high-profile species in and adjacent to the field included a Nutting's flycatcher, Boucard's wren, white-lored gnatcatcher, and dusky hummingbird. It was a great start for a beautiful day in Oaxaca.

As we walked back to the car, a lesser roadrunner crossed the lane just ahead of us. "Wow! look at that," I said. It does look like a smaller version of the greater roadrunner that occurs throughout much of the American Southwest." Later, we talked about that find as a huge surprise, a species that we had not thought might be at that elevation in the mountains.

Further along the highway, we drove through a pine-oak forest that had a surprising variety of habitats. Johnathan's guidebook stated that the common oaks of this zone included chestnut and netleaf oaks. As we continued up the slope, we found a pine woodland dominated by Michoacan and Chihuahuan pines. "This is the habitat where we might find a slaty vireo," I said. How about walking around and trying to find one?"

The slaty vireo is one of Mexico's endemic species that is rare and local, so we pulled off the road and began to wander about. After about 20 to 30 minutes, I detected a song just ahead of us that sounded to me like that of a vireo. But in spite of hearing the song, we could not find it. We continued up the highway, stopping at a number of other sites to see what we might find. At our very next stop, only about a mile further on, we did find our bird. It was well marked, with an overall slaty-gray plumage, a bright olive-green crown, wings and tail, and a white eye.

At another stop in a good patch of forest, we walked out to investigate and almost immediately we encountered a small flock of dwarf jays. A few minutes later, I was watching a happy wren. I tried to entice it closer for a better look, but with little success, but I noticed another little bird creeping through some weedy plants. It took me several seconds before I could see it well enough, and when I did, I shouted to Johnathan: "Johnathan, come here, here is a male cinnamon-bellied flower-piercer. A gorgeous bird!"

We stood there admiring this tiny black and deep-cinnamon bird with an upturned, hooked bill. It is the only small Mexican species with a such a characteristic. We watched it "snip" its way into the base of a small flower from which I assumed it extracted nectar. Johnathan's comment was, "What a neat little bird!"

Since that habitat looked especially productive, we wandered further from the highway, and before long we saw a little cabin hidden among some heavy vegetation. It looked deserted, but just being silly, I called out, "Hello, is anyone at home?"

Suddenly this huge figure walked out the broken-down door, and said, "I am, what do you want?"

Immediately I answered, "Nothing, we are just exploring the area looking at birds; sorry if we are disturbing you." The response was rather brusque and not very friendly: "Get on your way; leave me alone."

We hurriedly walked away from the cabin and back to our car. Afterwards, when Johnathan and I discussed the situation, we could not decide if that person in the forest was male or female. We only knew he or she was extremely rude. It wasn't until then that it dawned on us that the hermit that we had encountered spoke English. "I would love to know about that guy's history. Maybe he or she is in hiding from some nefarious happening."

About mid-day, we decided to continue into Oaxaca. We were so impressed with the birds we had found in the mountains that we decided to return after visiting Monte Alban. We knew that the mountains would produce many more species.

We were surprised at the city; it was a thriving and modern municipality. The city of Oaxaca sits within a broad valley at about 5,000 feet elevation along the eastern slope of the Sierra Madre de Sur. By the time we had acquired accommodations at the Mission de los Angeles, we did not have time to visit Monte Alban.

We decided to drive into the town center to experience the real Ciudad Oaxaca, to wander around the Plaza de Armas, and to eat at a nearby restaurant; we chose the El Paso. The central plaza, with its huge old trees, bandstand and walkways, was all I expected.

"Let's sit awhile outside the restaurant and watch the crowds" I said. Sitting there, drinking a cold cerveza was very relaxing.

We were pretty well left alone at first, but then we were approached by a gentleman carrying a huge pile of folded textiles, twice as high as he was. He placed his goods on the ground and asked in reasonably good English how much we would pay for a "beautiful Oaxacan rug?" I had no intention of buying a rug but asked if he also had serapes.

"Serapes? Sí, senor," he said, and he immediately selected a second piece, as beautiful as the first, and unfolded it for my inspection. But it was another rug.

I told him, "I am not interested in a rug, but would consider buying a serape."

With that, he told me that he had many serapes, and he laid out a third piece for our inspection. I could not help but show my admiration for that piece of art, but I again told him it was not a serape, and I would be interested only in a serape. He went through at least four more rugs before he admitted that all of the pieces he had for sell were rugs. Then he brought out a bird-decorated rug for inspection and asked how much I would give for that beautiful hand-woven rug.

I have never been one to drive a hard bargain, unless I really didn't care to buy. I decided to see just how far he was willing to go in negotiating for the bird rug.

"Senor," I said, "I am running low of money and I could not part with more than fifteen dollars."

The expression on his face was worth a dozen photographs. He informed me that he was supporting his elder mother, a wife, and five children, and that he could not possibly take less than forty dollars for the rug that he had worked so many hours to produce. He asked me to increase my price. Because he said, he knew that I liked his rug, and he would like me to have it.

My next price of seventeen dollars produced another pained expression, and he spent another ten minutes explaining how many hours it had taken him to weave the rug and how many people were depending upon him for their very survival. Then he said that he would ask me to pay his price and take it home.

I could barely stand the expression on his face when I told him, "Senor, I am not really interested in a rug, only a serape, and there is no way I could go over twenty dollars, and if you can't accept that price, I will walk away."

He looked at me for a long time, and I wondered if he was about to shout at me, or walk away, or something else. Suddenly, he said that he would take the twenty dollars but that he would have a very difficult time explaining to his family how he had given away his most beautiful rug. He added that the only reason he agreed on my price was because he knew that I would "admire his rug forever."

By the time we parted, he with my 20-dollar bill, and me with his gorgeous eight-by-five-foot rug, I was exhausted. But the Oaxacan rug salesman was correct. That bird rug became a subject of many conversations.

The following day, we set out to visit Monte Alban. Dawn found us wandering along the entrance road, which passed through a rather arid landscape. It was there along the roadside where we found one of our target birds, an Oaxacan sparrow. It was rather dull in appearance, but a new trip-bird, nevertheless.

After paying an entrance fee and buying a brochure, we entered the huge compound. Johnathan right away began reading from the brochure: "Monte Alban is Spanish for 'White Mountains,' and the ruins are located on a fifty-five-acre terrace plateau overlooking the Oaxacan valley. The immense hilltop ruins once were the cultural center of a city that encompassed an area of over fifteen square miles." He paused briefly and added, "The ruins were inhabited for more than twenty-five hundred years and served a succession of different peoples. Five distinct periods have been identified."

"According to the brochure," Johnathan continued, "the area was inhabited from as early as 4000 B.C., but construction of the city did not begin until approximately 500 B.C. Monte Alban reached its cultural peak during this period. The earliest sculptures depict distorted figures and facial features resembling jaguars, which represent Olmec traits."

"In other words," I said, "These ruins are older than any of those of the Mayan culture. That is amazing to me; I guess I thought that the Mayans were the earliest people to inhabit Mexico."

"But even at this early date, the Oaxacans represented a truly sophisticated society," Johnathan said. "They possessed a calendar, a writing system, and highly developed pottery. A second phase began at around 700 B.C., and lasted about three hundred years. It was then abandoned until the Zapotecs arrived. The Zapotec period, that lasted until about 700 A.D., was characterized by a tripartite social division of priests, clerks, and laborers. The city reached a maximum size of about sixty thousand inhabitants between 500 and 600 A.D. Following that period, the city began to decay. By 700 A.D., they were invaded by the Mixtecs from the northwest, who captured many of the Zapotec cites."

Johnathan added, "The Mixtecs were replaced by the Mayans in about 300 A.D., although their cities were not abandoned. It was the Mayans who contributed an observatory and a change in ceramic style. They also constructed a drainage system to channel and store water."

"But what happened to the Mayans," I asked.

Johnathan's response was unexpected. "They were gradually consumed by additional occupants, including the Aztecs. By 1586, the Aztecs established a military base there. Afterwards, Monte Alban was used more of a burial site for the Zapotecs and, later, the Mixtecs. More than 150 tombs from this later period have been uncovered."

All of this history was almost more than I could process, so I told Johnathan, "Let's visit the ruins. I want to see evidence of all this first-hand."

We began to explore portions of the Monte Alban compound. The ruins have been sufficiently restored so that anyone interested in the ancient ruins can appreciate what had been uncovered.

Much of the site had been restored to display the numerous stepped platforms and varied structures that are arranged on a north-south axis with two huge platforms at either end of an enormous sunken plaza. The platforms contained arrangements of pyramid-temples, palaces, patios and tombs. Structures along the edge of the great plaza include a ballcourt, without stone rings like we had seen at Palenque, and a pyramid with an internal staircase that is protected on both sides of the entrance by hieroglyphs of serpents and a man with a great headdress. Most of the buildings were plastered, and some had been painted and elaborated by current figures.

We found stelae and hieroglyphs throughout the ruins. "Many of these remind me of the stelae we saw at Palenque. But look at this one," I said. "That headdress looks like an ancient space helmet."

"I am told that some archeologists have claimed that these headdresses are actually depictions of helmets worn by extraterrestrials," Johnathan said. "There actually is a sect that visits Monte Alban annually to give voice to the idea that space people visit annually. So far, none of the extraterrestrials have been photographed."

"With what we are seeing, I guess I could almost join the sect. I wonder if they have dues?" I said with a chuckle. One of the very best stelae, located on the south platform, shows a jaguar wearing the headdress of the rain god, Coccijo. The stelae at the Platform of the Dancers seemed to depict stylized dancers engaged in a kind of ecstatic ritual. Some of Monte Alban's stelae are considered the oldest known written texts in the New World.

"Look at this one," Johnathan said, "interpreters of these writings have suggested that the figures, all of which appear lifeless, nude, and sexually mutilated, represent dead and tortured enemies. Other archeologists believe that they represent the ill and deformed, and that the structure was an early hospital.'

I could not help but think that the Monte Alban complex of stark stone structures, perched on a hilltop overlooking a more modern city and associated farmlands, offered a powerful sense of history and the mystery of human existence.

The following morning, we left the city very early, and by the time it became light enough to see our surroundings, we were high in the mountains, where we could watch the dawn creep into the canyons far below. As we progressed upward, we found numerous vistas where we admired the surrounding countryside. I was surprised at the number of tiny villages we could see from the highway, all scattered here and there below. We had not seen any of them along the lower highway.

We had stopped at one vista to survey the lower slopes when Johnathan said, "These mountains are filled with humanity." After a few minutes, he added: "I can count at least fifteen villages from this viewpoint. And from the number of cultivated fields, I imagine they are all farmers."

The higher ridges and plateaus were covered with coniferous forest. Several narrow, upland side-canyons provided a barranca-like environment with dense broadleaved vegetation.

Not too far from the highpoint of the highway, we stopped at a pull-out that was located near the bottom of a rather steep barranca that contained a good habitat of broadleaf vegetation and a trail that followed the bottom for several hundred yards. A short distance from the highway, we found a fruiting tree that I identified as a hackberry, and it was full of feeding birds. We backed away and sat a comfortable distance away, and watched what took place. Within less than an hour we had added a couple dozen bird species, many of which were new for our trip.

"Robert, there is an Aztec thrush. There are two. That is one species we have not seen yet." Indeed, and we sat there and admired that Mexican endemic. Before long we found several other species coming to feed on that one tree. We added a spot-crowned woodcreeper, tufted flycatcher, several rufous-backed robins, a ruddy-caped nightingale-thrush, crescent-chested and red warblers, chestnut-capped brush-finch, and collared towhee. But it was the red warbler that we admired most. It was a male that was a brilliant red color with a large snow-white patch just behind its eyes. "That bird will long be remembered, a truly classy little warbler."

When we tallied out list that evening at dinner, it included 84 species for the day, and 73 of those were lifers. Our birding in the Oaxaca mountains had been a marvelous success.

Instead of returning to Cuidad Oaxaca, we continued eastward toward Veracruz. There were several ruins that Johnathan wanted to visit along the Gulf Coast.

CHAPTER 13

VERACRUZ: CERRO DE LAS MESAS AND ZEMBOALA

B Y THE TIME we reached Taxtepec it was dark, but we had little trouble finding a room near the junction of Highways 175 and 147. We stayed at the Best Western, which had a restaurant. During dinner, we talked about the next several days. According to Johnathan's guidebook, the area around the city of Veracruz had a number of ruins. We knew that Veracruz was a huge city, and we did not want to spend any time in the city proper; we had hoped to find accommodations outside the city.

"If we stay along the southern edge of the city, at least the first night, we could visit Cerro de Las Mesas, that is near Puerto de Alvarado," Johnathan said. "In fact," he added, "Highway 175 goes right to Alvarado, and we could stay there."

"That sounds like a good plan to me. And since we will be close to the Gulf, I suspect that we could also find some birds that we have not seen yet."

By noon the following day, we had reached Alvarado. The city, with a population of about 50,000, was located along the Gulf, and a large lagoon – Laguna Alvarado -- was located to the west. Right away, I said, "This area looks to me like it not only might host an abundance of birds, especially waterbirds, but I also like the looks of the city."

"I agree," I said. "It looks clean and neat, and when we drove past the plaza, I thought it might be a good place to sit and enjoy the ambiance of the city.

"How about we get a room first, maybe at the Hotel Casa Blanca that we passed in town, and then see what kind of birds we can find along the coast and in the Laguna?"

Before long we were walking along the beach. The weather was beautiful, and the Gulf of Mexico was calm and full of waterfowl. Dozens of gulls, terns, and brown pelicans dominated the scene, but we were particularly interested in the shorebirds. Besides the widespread sanderlings, western and least sandpipers, dowitchers, and willets, we found three plovers – collared, snowy and Wilson's plovers - that were new for our list. Afterwards we walked along Laguna Alverado, where we found even more birds.

"There must be at least five thousand ducks out there; I wish I would have brought my spotting scope," I said. But just with binoculars we were able to identify 15 or more species." Closer to shore were black-necked stilts and American avocets. Suddenly Johnathan shouted, "Look, a northern jacana near the tules. That is a lifer for me." We spent several minutes admiring that long-legged, cinnamon bird with a black head and yellow bill.

After we got back to our room and showered, we drove into town, where we sat on a bench at the plaza and watched people. The citizens of Alverado were no different than any of other people we had watched during our trip. Before long, we walked down the street to find a restaurant. "Since we are on the coast, how about seafood," Johnathan said.

"Good idea. We haven't had a good fish dinner yet, and I'm ready." Just then two young ladies were walking by, and Johnathan said in Spanish, "Excuse me, we are trying to decide on a restaurant. We hope to have a good fish dinner. Can you recommend a restaurant?"

Although one of the ladies seemed extremely shy, the second one, that we learned was named Leilia, was not shy at all, and she and Johnathan immediately struck up a conversation. She first asked where we were from and what we were doing in Alverado. When Johnathan had answered her questions, she asked where we were going next. When Johnathan told her we planned to visit Cerro de La Mesas first and Quiahuiztlan later, she got excited and said, "My father is one of the guards at Cerro de La

Mesas. You must see him and tell him you have met his daughter. He will be your interpreter." In another few minutes, she asked, "Are either of you an archeologist; that is what I plan to study in university."

"No. Although neither of us are professional archeologists, I have been an amateur archeologist much of my life, and I am the one most interested in visiting as many of the ruins as possible. I suspect that Robert is finding the ruins fascinating. Maybe because many of the sites also possess good bird habitats."

When we finally got around to talking about a restaurant, Leilia said: "We were about to have dinner, too, and we would be honored to show you our favorite restaurant, La Lledgado de Pescador." We left the plaza and walked several blocks to the waterfront and the La Llegado de Pescador. We naturally invited Leilia and Nina to join us. The meal was excellent, and our friends were marvelous companions. Nina, once she relaxed, was also friendly and talkative. It was a thoroughly enjoyable dinner.

Afterwards, the four of us walked back to the plaza where we talked briefly before Leilia said, "We are to meet our friends here, and you are welcome to stay and meet them. One of them is courting Nina, and he may not appreciate it if he finds her with two Americans." That sounded like a warning to me, so we excused ourselves, and walked back to our car, and returned to our hotel.

Although we were aware of the numerous ruins surrounding Veracruz, it wasn't until we were back in our room and began to make decisions on an agenda for visiting a number of ruins during the next several days that we finally realized what that would entail; there are dozens of ruins within about a 50-mile radius. Although we had a guidebook that included all the principal ones, and an additional 30 or more, we wished that the guidebook listed them in some sort of priority according to their significance. For some unknown reason, we decided that we would visit Cerro de Las Mesas first, maybe because it was south of town. That way we could keep our room, at least until we decided to visit the numerous ruins north of the city.

Cerro de Las Mesa is located in the Papaloapan River Basin, about 30 miles from Veracruz. Cerro de Las Mesas, which means "Hill of the Altars," was occupied from 600 to 900 A.D., and was located on the western edge of what had once been the Olmec heartland. The compound is dominated by a series of low artificial mounds and a small man-made lake. Johnathan, in reading from the brochure we had purchased at the entrance, said, "In one of the mounds, archeologists found more than 800 jade items." As we wandered about, we found several steles. "Look at this large one," I said. "It depicts a man with a fancy headdress." We stood there a few minutes fantasizing about what all the features could mean. "The brochure points out that some of the features represent dates of occupation."

When we walked over to the lagoon, expecting to see some water birds, we found only a couple of least grebes. When we checking the tules on the edge, however, we found a great blue and a boat-billed heron. We admired the boat-billed heron. "That is one chunky bird; I can see why it was named boat-billed. Its bill is extremely wide, and it's black crown and white forehead give it a prominent appearance," I said. Then, just as we were about to leave the lagoon, Johnathan spotted two little ducks at the far end: "Robert, there are two masked ducks, far down the side by the tules." Sure enough! One more lifer.

Before noon we left Cerro de Las Mesas and drove back to Highway 180 and northward all the way to La Antigua. By then, we were hungry. We had eaten a granola bar at mid-morning at Cerro de Las Mesas, and we were ready for lunch. We ate an excellent lunch at Las Delicas del Mar and afterwards drove around town looking for a hotel. We got a room at the La Paloma. We had decided to stay in La Antigua because the next ruins – Zampoala – was only a few miles to the north.

We were impressed with the city. It appeared that the local folks were proud of their heritage. "According to the guidebook," Johnathan said, "La Antigua is the very first town settled by the Spanish in the New World." We found several very old buildings, including what the guidebook said was the first Catholic Church in the Americas, as well as a 16th Century house where the Spanish conqueror Hernan Cortez once lived. Although both of us were impressed with the history of La Antigua and agreed that the town was well named, we were anxious to see more ruins.

We ate breakfast at the hotel and were soon at the entrance to Zempoala. We paid a small entrance fee, purchased a brochure, and entered the compound. Just inside the entrance was a museum that we found to be well done. It also had a handy and clean restroom.

Zemboala means "place of the twenty waters," and the ruins are located where several rivers converged. When Johnathan began reading from the brochure, we learned that Zempoala, also known as Cempoala at the time of the Spanish Conquest, was the Totonac capital with a population of about 30,000 souls. It was the largest Mesoamerican center, and it was the place where Cortez met Xicomecoatl, also known as "Fat Chief," who later became an important ally.

Only a small portion of the main ceremonial area had been restored. "The majority of the buildings date from the 14th and 15th centuries," Johnathan said.

We discovered that all of the structures had been built on mounds to protect them from floods; the rivers flooded so often that all the structures were built so that they would remain above flood stage. "Americans should take a hint when building so many fancy homes in the floodplains," I said. "But I guess the insurance companies are able to take advantage of that ignorance."

The Great Temple is said to resemble the Temple of the Sun at Tenochtitán. The Temple of the Little Faces was decorated with stucco faces on the walls and with painted hieroglyphs on the lower sections. The Temple of Quetzalcoatl, dedicated to the feathered serpent god, was a square platform, but the Temple of Eheeatl, god of the wind, was round.

"Listen to this," Johnathan said, reading from the brochure, "Cortéz forged a union with the Totonac, and in 1519, Cortéz, his army, Totanac warriors, and 200 porters, set out from Zempoala for the Aztec capital of Tenochtitlan. That journey took them several months and included numerous victories along the way. Their route took them first to the high plateau of Tlaxcala and then to Cholula. Locals attempted to drive them back in both areas, but Cortez slaughtered all of the Aztec fighters he encountered. When he reached the heart of Tenochtitlan, Motecuhzoma II, the Aztec emperor, was conquered and enslaved."

Continuing to wander about the compound, we stopped at a number of other structures: a restored ballcourt, the Templo del Dios del Viento y la Cruz, dedicated to the god of the Winds, Templo Mayor, Templo de las Chimeneas, Temple of the Chimensy, and Circulo de los Gladiadores. "This temple certainly suggests the reverence the Totanac people had for their warriors," Jonathan said.

The Central Plaza is dominated by a massive pyramid containing intriguing rings of stones, each fashioned with rounded beach cobblestones, cemented together to form a series of small stepped pillars. The largest contained 40 of the stepped pillars. The brochure suggested that the rings were used to calibrate different astronomical cycles. Possibly, the Totanac priests were able to calibrate the movements of the moon closely enough to know when it might next be 'devoured.'

We wandered along the adjacent river, checking to see what birds might be present. Almost immediately I found a crane hawk, sitting in the high branches of sycamore tree. Instead of flying off, it sat there long enough that we were able to see it extremely well through our binoculars. We could clearly see its rather small body, tail with two white bands, and most notably its long red legs. After a few seconds later, Johnathan called out, "Here is a large woodpecker, I think it is a pale-billed woodpecker." Just as I found it high on the tree trunk, it gave a shrill call, and began its loud and rapid double taps, which continued for a good part of a minute before it flew down the river and out of sight.

As we continued along the riverway, we added a bronze-winged woodpecker, several Couch's kingbirds, a couple clay-colored robins, an Altamira oriole building a pendant nest, and an ivory-billed woodcreeper. Suddenly I was looking at an elegant trogon. We stood there for several minutes admiring that really special bird. It was a male, with an all green back, pale wing panels, coppery tail, black cheeks, and when it turned toward us, we saw its rosy-red belly. Truly a marvelous bird! Johnathan said, "I think that, for me, that is one of the most memorable of all the birds we have seen on this trip." Then, as if to impress us even more, it called out a rolling chatter, like "wehrr-rr-rr," and flew off to another tree along the waterway.

We spent most of the day at Zempoala, and in late afternoon drove back to town, stopped at our room long enough to shower and change clothes, and returned to the Las Delicas del Mar, where we had eaten the previous evening. As we sat down at our table, the same waitress asked us, in surprisingly good English, "How was your day? Did you see what you were looking for?"

"Yes, indeed," I answered. "We not only enjoyed the ruins but we also found several birds along the river."

"Oh, yes, are you also looking for birds? My brother is an expert on our birds. He would be pleased to help you find what you are looking for. If you want, I will call him to come to the restaurant, and he would be happy to tell you where you could find whatever birds you want to see."

"That would be wonderful," I said. "We would very much like to talk with your brother." She left us and immediately called her brother. When she returned to our table a few minutes later, she said, "My brother will come to the restaurant, and he will be pleased to talk with you about our birds."

We ordered, and before we had finished our meal, a tall, skinny kid appeared at the restaurant, and our waitress brought him to our table. My first impression of her brother was not a good one. He looked like a ten-year-old who could not possibly know where best to find birds. I was mistaken. I realized that he was not only wise about available habitats, but extremely knowledgeable about the local avifauna. His name was Ramón, and he sat with us for a long time, telling us about the area and the birdlife. We agreed to meet first thing in the morning so he could take us out to his favorite birding sites. Just as we were about to leave the restaurant, he asked, "Are you also interested in seeing owls?"

"Yes, indeed," I answered, "Do you know of where we might find owls?"

"Yes, I know where a mottled owl is nesting."

Off we went to find Ramón's mottled owl. It wasn't far out of town, along the edge of a wooded area. Seconds after we parked and began to walk across a field to where the nest was, a mottled owl flew over the field searching for prey. It flew to a fence post and perched there, allowing us to get a long look. It was light only from the full moon, but we were satisfied that it was indeed a mottled owl. So, instead of walking over to the nesting tree, we decided not to disturb the bird further.

The following morning, three of us walked along the edge of what looked like good tropical forest. But before we entered the forest, we found several birds of interest along the edge: several gray-crowned yellowthroats in brushy areas, both blue and varied buntings feeding right along the roadside, several tropical kingbirds flycatching from low shrubs, and an Audubon's oriole flying ahead of us. Just as we were about to enter the forest, a small buteo flew out from where it had been roosting. As it circled us, Ramón called out, "Short-tailed hawk!"

It circled directly above us, so we had an excellent look. As we were watching that hawk, a ferruginous pygmy-owl began calling from the fence-row on the far edge of the field. Before long, Ramón had called that pygmy-owl closer to us, and we had a surprisingly good look at that little owl. Ramón's imitated calls worked extremely well.

The forest was alive with birdsong. We spent the remainder of the morning in the forest, finding one bird after the other. Ramón knew his birds extremely well, and we were much impressed. Although most of the birds seen that morning had been seen earlier at other locations, we did add spot-breasted and white-bellied wrens, ivory-billed woodcreeper, lineated woodpecker, greyish saltator, and mostly importantly, a collared forest-falcon. We might have missed that bird if not for Ramón; he called it out, but it took me several minutes to find it perched high in the thick canopy. It was so well hidden, Johnathan had to help me find it. When I finally saw it, I was surprised that it had taken me so long, as it was a brilliant white underneath with a long white-banded tail and long yellow legs. But it was its head that impressed me most: a snow-white throat and collar and a peregrine-like head with a dark moustachial stripe. An outstanding bird!

That evening, we invited Ramón to eat with us. In spite of our first impression of him as being an uneducated young boy, he proved himself an extremely bright and personable young adult.

CHAPTER 14

VERACRUZ: QUIAHUIZTLAN AND EL TAJÍN

WE LEFT LA Antigua the next morning, heading north on Highway 180 to Quiahuztlan. After visiting Quiahuztlan, we planned to spend the night at Poza Rica, which is very close to El Tajín, our next stop. Quiahuiztlan, meaning "place of rain" in Nahuatl, is one of the Toltecs most beautiful sites. It is located on the Veracruzan coast very close to where Cortez and his small army landed in the New World in 1519. From there he formed a pact with 20 Totonac chieftains that gave him his first native alliance against the Aztec Empire.

My first impression of Quiahuiztlan was that it was dominated by a tall, massive basalt plug with sheer cliffs on three sides. The huge structure, known as "Penon de Bernal," had a trail to the summit. Later, after walking about the ruins, we climbed to the top where we were enchanted by the incredible panorama.

"What an amazing view," I said. "We can see for miles of the Veracruzan coastline from here. I can totally understand why the early people chose this area. A truly appealing location."

We parked at the top of a steep road and walked up to a ridge to where there were two tombs and the remains of an ancient Totonac tank for storing water. Johnathan, who was reading the brochure that we had purchased at the entrance, said, "These tombs look like miniature temples;

they even include a short flight of stairs." He added, "There is a tiny one-room sanctuary at the top of each."

Below the main terrace were two temples, called number one and number two, and a small plaza with an altar located in the center. Beyond the plaza was a small ballcourt and a cemetery that contained 23 small tombs.

"Everything, the ballcourt and these tombs are so small," I said. "I know that people in those days were much smaller than today, but the Toltecs who lived here must have been like midgets."

We found several monuments as we wandered around. Some were round, there were several pestle-like monuments of various sizes, but the one that caught our eye was a shark monument. "Does the brochure say anything about the Toltecs having some something special about sharks, or maybe they simply found shark meat especially delicious," I asked.

In a minute, he said: "Nothing that I can see, but it does emphasize the glyphs." We found the one displayed on the brochure. It was an intracavity carved cement boulder that had once contained various painted figures and symbols.

According to the brochure, Quiahuiztlan had its highest occupation from 900 to 1200, and the Totonic influence continued until the Spanish arrived and conquered the entire region. Cortez built a new town nearby that he named "Villa Rica de la Vera Cruz." It included numerous houses, a church, a market-square, and a small fortress.

There was little vegetation directly around the ruins, but when we climbed the Penon de Bernal, we could see mature forest in all directions except for the coastline, which was fringed with greenery. We found two birds of interest on our climb. We saw a gray hawk while climbing the steep slope; it was sitting on top of a small tree off to the right, and it allowed us an excellent view through our binoculars. When we reached the summit, a pair of red-billed pigeons flew out from the trees below; we must have walked right by them earlier.

Perhaps we saw the bird of the day after leaving the ruins. While driving back to Highway 180, we passed a large open field where we stopped to check on what birds might be present. Not more than 100 feet from the roadway were two double-striped thick-knees.

"Look at that," I yelled. "That is one bird I did not expect. They are nocturnal, and finding one at mid-day is a huge surprise."

We watched the closer bird for several minutes. It did not seem to be concerned about our presence, and we had a really good look. I was most impressed by its tall stature, bright yellow legs, and its distinct, broad white supercilium line. I opened my Mexico bird book, one of the few books I had brought with me, and read that thick-knees are a one-of-a-kind species of the unique family Burhinidae. A lifer for us both. We high-fived for our good luck.

We soon were back on the road, on our way to our next ruins, El Tajín. But, since we had eaten only a granola bar since breakfast, we stopped at the little town of Zaragoza, right on the coast, where we ate a shrimp cocktail and drank a soda. Although we had planned to drive all the way to Poza Rita, we stopped for the night at Nautla. As might be expected at a coastal town, we ate a fish dinner in a small restaurant looking over the Gulf.

Since we must have looked like two wandering vagabonds, we attracted attention at the restaurant. We soon were in a long conversation with two other vagabonds. Johan and Hans were German professors who were in Mexico to study linguistics. They were visiting several of the smaller villages along the coast, attempting to learn more about possible dialects resulting from the time of the Conquest. They apparently had discovered that many of the out-of-the-way villages spoke a unique dialect that they attributed to the time when the Spanish first arrived in the New World. They had also spent time in the Yucatan the previous year, where they had discovered unique dialects relating to the Mayan-Spanish interface there. I was intrigued by our conversation, and Johnathan and I talked about that discussion long afterwards.

Early the next morning, we were back on Highway 180 en route to Poca Rica and El Tajín. According to Jonathan's guidebook, El Tajín was one of the largest and, from 600 to 1200, one of the most important cities of the Classic Toltec era. Knowing that it would likely take a considerable amount of time to adequately explore the site, we rented a room in Poca Rica, meaning "rich well," for the night. The Fiesta Inn provided access to town and the route southward to El Tajín. By the time we got a room, it was late afternoon, so we decided to drive around the city. Until then, I had not realized that Poca Rica was a large city with a population of more than 200,000. It is an "oil town" founded in 1957 by PEMEX, but since then the 'rich well' had partially dried up. We were impressed, however, how well the city was laid out with large boulevards and a well-maintained city park. Rather than immediately searching for a restaurant, we stopped near the park and sat on a bench where we could watch the people and absorb some of the ambiance of the city.

The park itself was very pretty with numerous tall trees, a number of maintained flowerbeds, and a small pond. Almost immediately, we saw a number of birds feeding in the trees. Most were birds we had already recorded on our trip, including several species of orioles, a couple of tanagers, clay-colored robins, and tropical kingbirds. I found a pair of flame-colored tanagers feeding alongside the robins. Johnathan and I saw them at the very same time, and we called out "flame-colored tanagers!" simultaneously. The male was a beautiful bird with a bright red head and breast, and a pair of white wing-bars.

While staring at the tanagers, we suddenly realized that we had attracted a small crowd that was standing around us trying to understand what we were looking at. In the crowd was a young lady, about our age, who said, "I see you are birders, and you are watching the *tangara dorsirrayada*, the bright red tanager." Both Johnathan and I were surprised that here was someone who knew the birds. Soon began a conversation about her interest in birds and the surroundings. She introduced herself as Maria and her friend as Carmalíta. They were students from Mexico City, who were there to study changes in the human population after the decline in the local oil industry. Both women had grown up in Poca Rica and spoke very good English.

After a rather long conversation about odds-and-ends, I asked if they knew of a good nearby restaurant. Without any hesitation, Maria said that the El Tajín directly across the street from the park was excellent. So, naturally, we invited the women to join us. It was very obvious, once we entered the restaurant, that everyone there knew Maria and Carmalíta; we learned later that Maria's father owned the El Tajín. Because of that, perhaps, we got special attention, and Maria said, "Please, let me order. I will order for all of us, and I know that you will love the food." And we did! My meal was excellent. Maria said that the dishes she ordered were her grandmother's secret recipes, and she added, "Even I am unable to pry the recipes from my grandmother. She told me that she will give them to me when I marry. But I am afraid that may be a long time."

Carmalíta made a comment that surprised me. "You know, my dear friend, that you already would have those recipes if you had agreed to marry Jónas. He loves you and will continue to court you until you say yes."

Neither Johnathan or I knew what to say, so neither of us said anything. Maria did not answer, although she seemed embarrassed.

We spent another hour in the restaurant, but it soon got very busy; I had forgotten that most Mexicans eat their evening meals much later than most families do in the United States.

Before long, Maria suggested that we take a walk. We left the restaurant and soon were walking around the park. The four us made up a small contingent among the dozens of other young folks strolling in the park. By now we had paired up to a degree that Maria was holding my hand and Carmalíta and Johnathan were also holding hands. Eventually, we found an empty bench where we sat side by side and side by side. It was a beautiful night; there was a full moon, and I felt very amorous; I missed Carol and the relationship we once had.

Maria asked me if I had a girlfriend, and why I was not yet married. I explained that I did not have a full-time girlfriend, that I had not yet met the right one, and I wanted to see more of the world. I turned to Maria and asked, "How about you? You are a beautiful woman; I can't believe you are not yet married."

"I too am not ready. As Carmalíta suggested, I have had a long-time admirer, but I do not feel the same." She then added, "Maybe I will meet someone else. I think that I would know right away."

"I know that you will do the right thing," I said. "I believe that you are mature enough to recognize what that right thing is, when it occurs." In another few minutes, I added, "It is getting late and we have a full day ahead of us. If you are at the restaurant tomorrow evening, we can talk some more."

"Robert, I hope that someday I can find a man like you, someone whom I can love and be loved equally."

Later, when Johnathan and I returned to our room, I told him about that conversation. He looked at me for a long time and then said, "Robert, you have a very special something that makes women trust you. I know that you will be very successful in life. I admire you a great deal."

I did not know what to say. I have always thought of myself as a very average person, able to talk with almost anyone, but never to the extent that the few women I have known were more than just friends. Afterwards, I lay in bed a long time thinking about our conversation.

It was then that I realized that I had almost constantly been thinking of Carol. I knew that I would not sleep with Maria, even if she came to my bed. I truly was in love with Carol.

By morning, all we could think about was El Tajín. Johnathan was most interested in visiting ruins, but I also was getting hooked on the Mayan, Toltec and Aztec cultures doing as well. I found El Tajín to be especially fascinating.

The main city of El Tajín is defined by two streams, which merge to form the Tlahuanopa Arroyo, a tributary of the Teotihuacan River. The entire city was surrounded by rainforest and low rolling mountains that gave it an appearance of being in a great valley. The region is very intriguing. Right from the start, I was eager to explore the forest.

On entering the compound, we had purchased a brochure, and Johnathan was soon telling me about the ruins. "El Tajín, which means "thunder and lightning bolt," was one of the largest Gulf Coast cities, at more than twenty-six hundred acres. It was the most important city of the Classic era from 600 to 1200. It was the center of trade for the entire Gulf Coast. But from 1230 to 1785, the city experienced a gradual decline. During its peak, however, it contained numerous temples, palaces, pyramids and ballcourts." He added: "In spite of its size, the Spanish conquerors did not become aware of its existence until much later. It reached its peak after the fall of Teotihuacan."

We learned that El Tajín was occupied as early as 5600 B.C., first by nomadic hunters and gathers and eventually by sedentary farmers. It was subordinated by the Olmec culture around 1150 B.C., and later by the Toltecs, but it is unclear who built the city. It was later deserted for over 500 years, allowing the jungle to reclaim the area. Today, only about fifty percent of the structures have been uncovered and studied. In spite of that, the site was declared a World Heritage Site as early as 1923. That designation was principally due to its unique architecture, especially its decorative niches and its cement forms, which are not found elsewhere.

The best known of the El Tajín structures is the Pyramid of the Niches, but other important structures include the Arroyo Group, the North and South Ballcourts, and the Palace of Tajín Chico. The compound includes 20 ballcourts, the last three not discovered until 2013. Two of the ballcourts contain sculptured panels that depict the ballgames and their spiritual significance. The South Ballcourt panels show images of underworld deities and a player being decapitated. On seeing that panel, Johnathan said, "According to the brochure, sacrifices were done to allow the losers to approach the gods and to ask for pulque for the people."

"I find that weird. If that was the case, that was a very strange method of worship. Probably, the pulque was used as a way to anesthetize the player being killed."

"I'll bet that the priests drank more pulque than those being sacrificed."

We stood in front of the Pyramid of the Niches for a long time, admiring the odd-looking seven-story structure. "Look at that panel," Johnathan said. "It shows a ceremony being held at a cacao tree. Fascinating! Religion at El Tajín was based on the movement of the planets, the stars, and the sun and moon."

We did not, however, find a tower like that at Palenque, where it could have been used to study the heavens. When I mentioned that, Johnathan said, "Maybe a tower was not necessary. Without surrounding lights, the stars would be amazing!"

It was late afternoon by then, and we decided to postpone our forest visit until the next day. By the time we reached our room at Poca Rica, it was dinnertime. We showered and drove into town to eat at the El Tajín restaurant again. Waiting for us at a table were Maria and Carmalíta, both looking beautiful. I almost forgot about our great day in the ruins, and had an urge to get to know Maria on a more personal basis. Although it may have been my imagination, but I believed that Maria was feeling the same toward me.

But it was not to be, at least that evening. Just as we were finishing dinner, Senor Guzman, Maria's father walked into the restaurant and came directly to our table. I wasn't sure what he thought about his daughter being with two Americans, although he seemed congenial and pleasant, and he even paid for our dinners. He told Maria that he had come to the restaurant to tell her that her mother was ill and asking for her. Soon afterwards Senor Guzman, Maria and Carmalíta left the restaurant. Johnathan and I sat there for a few more minutes and then left for our room at the La Fiesta where we talked about what birds we might find in the forest the next morning.

Dawn the next morning found us at the edge of the El Tajín forest. And what a morning it was! Birdsongs emanated from every direction. Even before we entered the forest, we recorded several blue-black grassquits and white-collared seedeaters along the roadway. As we continued walking along the edge of forest, we found a number of species that were out in open, feeding on the abundant flying insects. Key birds that morning along the edge of the forest included a masked tityra, spot-breasted wren, white-breasted wood-wren, golden-crowned warbler, and a yellow-throated euphonia. The bright morning sunlight gave them all a wonderful glow.

Just as we started into the forest, an owl, that had been perched further down the forest edge, suddenly flew out into the open, only about 100 feet from where we were standing. It landed on the ground and captured a small rodent, pinned it down, and then flew back into the forest, carrying its prey. "That was an owl," I cried. "Did you see it well enough to identify it?"

"Yes, I saw it, but I am not sure what species it is." We began to describe to each other what we had seen, and before long we were sure it was a screech-owl. We agreed that it was heavily streaked with dark brown. "And," I added, "it had a series of white wing-spots." We opened the bird book and began to determine the species. After about 20 minutes, we agreed that we had just witnessed a vermiculated screech-owl. "A great bird for the new day!" When we entered the forest, we found that the birdsong had not diminished. One of the first birds we saw was a blue-crowned motmot that we admired from only about 30 feet distance. Before long we identified two woodcreepers, spot-crowned and olivaceous, both spot-breasted and white-bellied wren, and a lineated woodpecker moving around on a tall tree-trunk trying to hide from us. The bird of the morning was a rose-breasted becard. Not only did we have a really look at it, but Johnathan found its pendant nest hanging on a tree branch about 15 feet about the ground.

That morning we recorded 64 species, of which all but eight were lifers for me. It was a highly successful morning.

By late morning, when the peak of the morning chorus had subsided, we were wandering through the forest admiring the diversity of the vegetation. One of the most distinctive features of a rain forest is its dense canopy, which exists between 30 and 150 feet above the forest floor. Except at openings, the habitat forms a closed system of intertwining limbs and vines that provide arboreal pathways that are every bit as important as those on the ground.

A multilayered forest, such as the one we were observing, offered distinct habitats for various birds as well as other creatures such as salamanders, amphibians, reptiles, and mammals. Even the abundant bromeliads provided an additional niche where hummingbirds and a few other species can find water and nectar.

I found our afternoon activities studying the vegetation and observing birds totally enjoyable. By late afternoon it was time to head into town and maybe meet up with Maria and Carmalíta again.

Once in the restaurant, only Carmalíta was there, sitting at the same table from the night before. She quickly explained that Maria's mother was ill and that she needed to stay with her mother. When I attempted to learn more, Carmalíta would only say that her absence was also due to the fact that Maria's father had already selected a husband for her and would not allow any distractions from what he planned for his daughter.

Later, Johnathan and I talked about that kind of behavior, knowing that it was not unusual in Mexico, at least in much of the country. "I understand that culture," I said, "but if such a practice continues, there eventually will be considerable rebellion by young women."

Johnathan responded, "I imagine that changes already are taking place in many parts of Mexico. I read once that the women in Mexico City and some of the other large cities are much freer from such practices. I suspect that freedom will eventually spread throughout the country."

"I think it will, but cultural changes are slow, and we may not be around to see such changes."

After that exchange, we began to discuss the next few days. We were ready to get into the interior of the country, although we were not looking forward to the necessity of being in Mexico City, one of the most polluted cities in the world. But if we were to see Tenochtitlan, the center of the Aztec Empire, it would be necessary.

CHAPTER 15

ZEMPOALA AND POPOCATÉPETL

THE NEXT MORNING, we checked out of the La Fiesta and were soon on our way to Zempoala. It felt good to be heading west into the interior. Once away from the coast, we were in farming country, and we soon realized that the terrain was very slowly gaining altitude.

We reached Huachimango by late morning and decided to have lunch before continuing on to Zempoala. We chose a rather quaint restaurant near the plaza. Our waitress was a middle-aged lady who barely spoke any English, but Johnathan was able to order for us and to carry on a conversation. By now, I could speak some Spanish, but only enough to order a meal and get a room; if it was necessary to ask directions, I probably would have gotten lost.

As so often is the case at restaurants in Mexico, our waitress asked where we were from and what we were doing in Huachimango. I had begun to realize that those questions were not snoopy, but honest friendly inquiries. Of course, she and Johnathan were soon carrying on a conversation about where we were from, what we were doing in Mexico, and our intention of visiting Zempoala. Our meals were tasty but very spicy. By now I had begun to appreciate spicy food, at least more so than our first Mexican meals several weeks ago.

After lunch we continued south on Highway 138, past the city of Tulancingo and on toward Mexico City. When we arrived at the junction of Highways 138 and 2, the route around Mexico City, we decided that, instead of getting closer to the big city, we would get a room in Cuidad Cahagun, located close to the Zempoala ruins. We stayed overnight at Hotel Los Balcones del Camino, close to the city center.

Before dinner, we drove to the Central Plaza, as we had done on several other occasions. We found a bench and began watching people. It was too early in the evening to experience the typical parade of young people walking about, but the plaza was busy nonetheless. We left the bench and walked around the Plaza; it is large, encompassing several blocks. We passed a section that had been planted with a wide a variety of flowering plants, and we circled the garden to see what birds might be present.

"Look, a hummingbird," I said as I saw it feeding on one of the flowering shrubs.

"What is it," Johnathan said. It remained for only a few minutes before it zoomed away.

"What did you see; let's try to identify it," I said. We tried to figure it out, but we couldn't be sure because we had left our bird book in the hotel. "It had a red throat like a ruby-throat, but it is larger, and I also saw a white line on its cheek." Later, back in our room, we decided that we had seen an amethyst-throated hummingbird. It was a new bird for us both of us; a good beginning for our central Mexico sightings.

The ruins of Zempoala were just north of town a few miles, so by early morning we had paid a small entrance fee, purchased a brochure, and entered. Zempoala, which means "place of waters," is also known as Cempoala. According to the brochure, its name refers to the sophisticated irrigation system the city once had, although little more than ditches remain. Several structures, however, did remain, although only a few had been uncovered, excavated, and studied.

The most impressive structure at Zempoala is Tempo la Mayor, although it still was partially covered with vegetation. "Tempo la Mayor," Johnathan read, "was once covered with white plaster that Cortez, on seeing it in 1519 for the first time, thought, because it gleamed brightly in the sunshine, that it was pure silver. So," Johnathan added, "Cortez placed a cross at the top. And to commemorate that event, he had Mass said by a Catholic priest."

It was in Zempoala where Cortez made an alliance with the Toltec leader, Chicomacatl, who was dubbed "Fat Chief" by his people because of his enormous girth. Zempoala, during that period of time, was considered the capital of the Totonac peoples. Cortez also discovered that the Toltecs were "bloody" people. One of his men, Bernal Diaz, wrote that "every day they sacrificed three to five Indians, and offered their hearts to their idols." It also is said that Cortez destroyed all the idols he found and that he 'had the main temple cleaned and refurbished, and put in place a cross and an image of the Virgin Mary.'

We spent most of the day at Zempoala. Although the ruins were not as extensive and readily available as those at Palenque, Tikal, and some other sites we already had visited, we nevertheless enjoyed the day. At mid-elevation, it was cooler and less humid than the sites closer to the Gulf. And it was not as crowded, in spite of being so close to Mexico City.

We did find a number of birds as we wandered about the ruins. The most exciting bird was an American kestrel that was perched atop Tempo la Mayor when we first arrived.

"Johnathan," I said, "that little falcon has long been one of my most favorite raptors. I have long admired its contrasting features. Look at its rusty plumage and black-and-white facial pattern." As we were watching, it flew from the top of the temple and dove to the ground, not more than 50 feet from we were standing, where it pounced on its prey. It hit a horned lark, pinned it down briefly, and then flew back to its perch with the lark held tightly in its talons. We stood there in admiration and watched it tearing feathers off its prey. And within another three to four minutes, it had torn the lark into pieces and swallowed each one.

Later, while eating dinner, we talked about the next several days. Although our next goal was to visit Teotihuacan, located on the edge of Mexico City, we both would like to see more of the countryside. We already had agreed that we would head for home after visiting Tenochtitian, our last planned ruins.

It was Johnathan who came up with another idea that I immediately agreed with. "How about seeing some the Central Mexican high-country? I would love to get into the upper slopes of Popocatépetl or Iztaccíhuatl. Those two peaks are only a couple hours to the southwest of us. What do you think?"

I was truly excited about that idea. "Johnathan," I said, "That is one super idea!"

The next morning found us driving south to Highway 150 and west to Texmelcun, then west to Chalco, and south to Amecmeca. I was driving, and Johnathan was reading from the guidebook, which contained an extensive section on Mexico's Sierra Volcánica Transversal, the mountain range just ahead of us that contains several of the highest peaks in Mexico. "The highest is Pico de Orizaba, or Chitaltrepetl, a Nahua Indian word meaning 'Mountain of the Star.' At 18,851 feet in elevation, Orizaba is the third highest mountain in all of North America. Only Alaska's Denali, at 20,320 feet, and Canada's Mount Logan, at 19,850 feet, are higher."

"How high are Popo and Izta? From what we see from a distance, they must be in the same general range of elevations."

"They are," Johnathan said. "Popo is 17,781 feet and Izta is 17,343 feet in elevation. They both are Nahuatl words, meaning Smoking Mountain and Naked Lady, respectively. Plus, Nevado de Toluca, or Xinantecatl, meaning 'Naked Man,' is 15,001 feet, and the fifth highest is Malinche, or Malantzin, at 14,637 feet elevation." Johnathan added, "Malinche was named for a female Mayan guide, interpreter and concubine of Cortez."

"That is amazing stuff! I bet that the vast majority of people that visit Mexico know almost nothing about the mountains. I suspect that most people who visit Mexico are interested only in its sunny beaches and spicy food" I said.

"Here's something more," Johnathan said. "It is well known that most of Mexico's highest peaks are inactive volcanoes, but new volcanoes are not unusual within the region. It says here that a farmer, plowing his field two hundred miles west of Mexico City, watched as a fissure opened in the ground and volcanic material poured out. The new volcano was three feet high the following morning, four hundred and sixty feet high one week later, and had risen to a height of thirteen hundred feet by the time it stopped flowing."

"That is hard to believe. It seems to me that this region of Mexico is just as active as some areas in the Hawaiian Islands," I said.

The paved road beyond Amecameca begins at the plaza and has signs pointing to Buena Vista and Popo-Izta National Park. The mountain scenery above Amecameca was spectacular. Izta is on the left and forms a massive ridge that, with just a little imagination, resembles the body of a recumbent female figure, complete with head, breast, and knees. To the right is Popo, a single conical-shaped peak that reminds one of Mount Hood or Mount Rainier in the Cascade Range of the Pacific Northwest.

Our route continued upward for about 20 miles to Tlamacas, park headquarters at 12,800 feet above sea level.

Tlamacas is the center of activities for the Popocatépetl-Iztaccíhuatl National Park with a very nice, modern stone lodge, complete with overnight accommodations and a restaurant. Park headquarters is located across a stone plaza from the lodge and contains a climbing office where everyone who climbs either Popo or Izta must register. We were able to acquire a room for the night, and we also registered for a hike up the slope of Popo for the next day. Our permit allowed us to climb only to the lower edge of the snow pack. In spite of it being mid-summer, Popo receives more snow in summer than it does in winter because the warm lowlands produce more moisture in summer than in winter, resulting in a greater amount of rain and snow at high elevations.

We had stopped several places along the lower roadway to see what birds might be available. Just above the Amecameca-Buena Vista junction is a picnic area where we stopped to check out what birds might be present. Almost immediately we found an ocellated thrasher. "That," I said, "is one of Mexico's many endemic birds, a really good find."

We walked along the roadside that passed through a forested area, where we found buff-breasted, pine and tufted flycatchers, a blue mockingbird, and a rufous-capped brush-finch. Johnathan suddenly shouted, "Robert, come look at this little colorful bird; I think it's a blue-hooded euphonia!" And what a gorgeous bird it was. We spent several minutes standing there admiring its bright turquoise cap and neck, contrasting black face, and cinnamon belly.

Other birds recorded that day along the forest edge and fence-rows included a Strickland woodpecker, a white-eared hummingbird, a flock of bushtits, clay-colored robins, fan-tailed and golden-crowned warblers, a slate-throated redstart, and Sierra Madre and striped sparrows. In addition, we kept hearing songs that reminded me of junco songs. It took several minutes until I was sure; it was a yellow-eyed junco, singing a rapid song that was repeated over and over again.

The highest portion of the Tlamacas roadway transects the boreal forest and provides easy access to the highland environment. There is a three-way junction at the Paso de Cortez, 14 miles above Amecameca. The pass is situated midway between Popo and Izta and is named for Hernan Cortez. Cortez who, with his Spanish army, crossed these mountains at this point on their November, 1519 march from Veracruz to Tenochtitlan. The battle that ensued soon afterwards marked the beginning of the end of the Aztec Empire.

We stopped at the pass, climbed out of our car and walked up and down the road, looking for whatever birds we could find. Brown-throated wrens were the most vocal from the brushy roadsides, and in the surrounding forest, we found a gray-banded wren, Mexican chickadees, white-breasted and pygmy nuthatches, and red and olive warblers. We admired the red warbler for several minutes as it sang high, thin chips and short, accelerating trills that ended with an upward inflected note. We also spent several minutes watching the gray-barred wren. "This wren is one of the largest members of the wren family; it is very similar to the cactus wren of the southwestern deserts in the U.S." I said.

Stopping at another spot along the highway, we added a russet nightingale-thrush, two fan-tailed warblers, and a number of striped sparrows. The most unexpected species at that location was a Sierra Madre sparrow. I had to look several times before I was sure. It looked to me like a mix between a song sparrow and a hermit thrush. "Johnathan" I said, "Look at the sparrow along the roadside ahead of us. That is a Sierra Madre sparrow; it is endemic and I have heard that it is one Mexico's rarest birds. A great find."

In spite of the high altitude, neither of us seemed to be bothered. Being birders instead of sprinters, we moved slowly and stopped whenever we had an opportunity to watch birds. The one exception occurred near the pass when we found a small mammal crossing the road ahead of us. "It's a weasel," I said, and we both ran down the road, hoping that it had stopped so we could get a better look, but by the time we reached the spot on the road where it had crossed, we were breathing hard, and we had missed the weasel. We compared what we had seen, and we soon agreed that it had been a long-tailed weasel.

Our hike on Popo was spectacular. The day was cool and bright, the sky was unbelievably blue, and the forest was bright green. We added only a few birds to our list: Steller's jay, common raven, brown creeper, and brown-backed solitaire. We heard the solitaire long before we finally found one and realized that we had been hearing several during our hike. Its song has been described as an 'accelerating, squeaky, metallic, jangling series, beginning hesitantly before running into a jumbled crescendo.' We eventually saw one, high on a conifer tree, that required our binoculars to see it well.

When we reached the snow-line, we were forced to turn back, but we were fully satisfied that we had experienced the best of Popocatépetl.

It was nearly dark when we returned to our room at Tlamacas. As we were preparing to go to dinner, we realized that we were extremely tired. "This altitude has had a real affect on me," Johnathan said. I agreed fully. Both of us live at much lower elevations, and the high altitude had taken a toll, but we seemed to recover soon after we walked into the restaurant.

Although most of the dozen or so tables were already taken, we were seated next to two truly beautiful ladies. We soon were talking about our day on the mountain, how long we had been in Mexico, and where we lived. Both Margery and Carolina were students at Sacramento State in California, and they were travelling in Mexico 'just to experience a foreign country.'

It was also soon apparent that they were equally interested in men; they were not just flirtatious, but reeked of desire. The tiredness that I felt before dinner evaporated while talking with Margery and Caroline. It did not take a great deal of persuasion to invite them to share our beds for the night.

I must admit that I thoroughly enjoyed that night of passion, but I had never before ended up in bed with the opposite sex so fast and with so little foreplay. And the more I thought about that night, I felt only guilt and remorse; my true love was Carol.

The next day at breakfast, Johnathan told me that Caroline admitted that, besides wanting to climb Popo, they planned to sleep with as many men as possible during their trip. I knew that Margery had initiated the conversations and the actions that ended in my bed, but I did not realize until then that they, in a sense, had manipulated us right from the start. I felt almost violated, but on the other hand, I had enjoyed the sex.

As much as we hated the idea of going into the Mexico City region, we left Tlsamacas soon after breakfast and headed to Tenochtitian. But instead of going directly into the city, we had decided to first visit the

Tula ruins that lay to the north of Mexico City. We retraced our route to Cuidad Sahagun, past the Zempoala area, to Tula de Allende. In Tula de Allende, a town of about 28,000 people, we drove around town to find a hotel that could provide access to the central plaza and restaurants. We chose the Hotel Posada Tolteca, probably because we liked the name more than anything else.

When we checking into the hotel, Johnathan asked the lady which of the local restaurants she would recommend. She told us that her favorite was the nearby Las Mesites Comida Artesanal. Before eating, however, we walked to the plaza, found a bench, and began watching the people.

CHAPTER 16

TULA

WE DID NOT go directly to Mexico City, but, learning that nearby Tula had ruins, we skirted the big city and, by late afternoon arrived in Tula de Allende. It was a clean and neat town and the streets are wide and well maintained. Flowering plants bloomed along the streets and in every corner or opening available. It was a lovely town. We found a hotel near the town center that was a convenient and comfortable place to stay.

We began our evening at the plaza, where one of the first thing I noticed was the smell of flowers. The local folks seemed better dressed than in some of the other towns we had visited. They all seemed happy and excited. We soon learned that the whole town appeared to be preparing for a celebration of some sort.

We sat there for only a few minutes before a small group of girls, all high-school age or younger, approached us with smiling faces. "Are you here for the wedding?" one of the girls asked. "Are you related to Johnny? I am told that several of his American friends have been invited."

We learned that Johnny was to marry a local girl, Corrína Músquiz, the next day, and that the whole town was celebrating, and we were invited to a pre-wedding dance at the Catholic Hall that night. When Jonathan asked about the location of the dance, one of the girls pointed down the street to where we could see a number of banners and a lighted sign announcing the big event. Before we could ask anything more, the girls marched off toward the hall.

"I guess we are invited," Johnathan said. "As excited as that group of girls were, I wonder if they are really able to extend us an invitation?"

"I'll never turn down a party. You can bet, as jubilant as they were, and as excited as everyone else we have seen is, we would hardly be noticed." I added: "You never know, we might even find two lovely ladies who would help us enjoy the evening."

The party that evening was a marvelous affair. My guess was, if we were even noticed, that everyone assumed we were Johnny's friends from out of town. We learned that Johnny was an American who was attending the University of Florida, where he met Corrína, who also was a student at the university. They had fallen in love, and they were about to be married in Corrína's home town of Tula de Allende.

There was an enormous amount of food and drink at the party. Just when I finished one drink, a hostess was there to hand me another. The drink was a tequila punch, margaritas, and considerably stronger than any alcohol I had drunk any time in the past. It was almost midnight before the real party began in earnest. Although I had never drunk more than a couple rum punches back home on St. Croix, I discovered that, with only a couple margaritas, I could easily lose track of my senses. I needed to eat something from the buffet. And what a layout of food it was!

I never before had tasted such delicious food. I was most impressed with the pork that was dripping with a delicious sauce, and the bar-b-que shrimp was unbelievable. I later wondered if the food was as good as I thought, or if it was largely a result of too many margaritas.

Johnathan and I sat at a side table eating when a rather heavy-set gentleman rose up from the head table and began to speak. I soon learned that this was Corrína's father. He welcomed everyone and expressed his sincerest desire that everyone should eat and drink as much as desired, and began a speech about how happy he was to give his daughter away to such a marvelous individual. He added that he hoped that he would soon become a grandfather. There was great clapping and laughing at that. The applause gave him additional momentum, and he continued his speech.

One of my tablemates, a lovely young lady by the name of Chloe, told me that Mr. Morales, Corrína's father, was extremely wealthy, and he was the one paying for the grand celebration. I also leaned that Mr. Morales was giving the newly married couple a ten-day, all-expenses honeymoon trip to France.

Neither Chloe or I paid much attention to Mr. Morales' speech after the first 20 minutes or so, and we soon were talking about Johnathan and me and what we were doing in Mexico. Chloe told me that she had never before been in Mexico, but had spent her whole life in Florida. "Robert," she said, "You men are able to travel wherever and whenever you can, but my parents are so strict that they would never allow we to travel without a guardian. Even here, my aunt has accompanied me. I love my aunt, but I am too confined."

I told Chloe about my aunt and Uncle Gus in Miami, what had happened during my short stay with them, how I had met Johnathan, and how that resulted in visiting Mexican ruins and ending up in Tula de Allende. The conversation lasted for the remainder of Mr. Morales' speech.

"What are your plans after tonight?" she asked.

"Tomorrow we plan to visit the Tula ruins, and sooner or later see the Aztec ruins in Mexico City," I responded. "My aunt and I plan to spend two more days in Tula, and I know she would like to visit those ruins; she studied

Mexico history in college. Would you and Johnathan consider us going with you?"

"I would need to ask Johnathan first, but I can see no reason why not. The idea of spending the day with you and your aunt, especially someone who has studied Mexico history, would be great."

Chloe and her aunt, Maya, were also staying at the Hotel Posada Tolteca, and we planned to meet for breakfast at the hotel before going to the Tula ruins.

And what a day it was! Maya was a joy! Not only was she knowledgeable about the Tula ruins but the entire history of Mexico as well, and she also had a wonderful personality and a great sense of humor. When I asked her about her name, she explained that she had changed it from Margaret in her teens after visiting the Mayan ruins in the Yucatan.

"So," I asked, "are you an expert on the Mayans as well as the Aztecs?"

"No, I just didn't like Margaret. Don't you like Maya better, too? I thought about Minnie or Goofy, but I liked Maya better."

Even before we entered the Tula compound, Maya was telling us about the Toltec culture and its relationship with Cortez. "Cortez arrived on the nearby coast in the spring of 1519. Although he did not face any aggression from the Toltecs, there was conflict within his own troops. Many of his army were eager to return to Spain, so he destroyed all his ships so that his soldiers could not go back."

"That should have sent a message allright. I imagine it also told his soldiers that they were going forward. Did Cortez know what was ahead of them?'

"Yes and no. He learned a good deal about what he was likely to find from the local Toltecs, and he sent spies ahead. He worked out an arrangement with the Toltecs, who had long been enemies of the Aztecs. So, with his army of 500 or more Spaniards and as many as 200,000 reinforcements, they moved on, destroying all the small village temples along their route."

"I wonder what he thought when he discovered the high mountains in front of him? I am sure that his Toltec friends were aware of the dangers. Crossing those mountains must have been a real challenge."

"Undoubtedly, but by then it was spring and much of the lower slopes were free of snow. But nevertheless, it took more than two months to reach Tenochtitlan. Historians tell us that many of his soldiers deserted, but he prevailed. I can't imagine what he thought when he first looked into the valley of Mexico and saw the great island city of Tenochtitlan."

"I am curious how Tula fits into the story, I said. "It is considerably north of Tenochtitlan."

"Yes, it is," she answered. "It is one of many cities that Cortez conquered, but much later than his defeat of Tenochtitlan."

"Before the fall of Tenochtitlan," Maya continued, "Tula paid homage to the Aztec nation, but after the defeat, Tula rose to prominence, and Tula became known as the 'City of Warriors.' Although It had long been an important regional center as the legitimate capital of the Toltec Empire and an important center for trading, Tula had reached its greatest power between 900 and 1150, when it had a population of about 60,000 souls. One of its greatest assets at the time were nearby obsidian mines. Because of obsidian, used for arrow and spear points, Tula became an important trading center, and Tula obsidian has been found as far off as Costa Rica."

We entered the Tula compound, where our first stop was the Jorge R. Acosta Museum, a modern structure that not only tells about the history of Tula, but also contains numerous artifacts that had been discovered during various excavations. One of the interpretive panels in the museum described the location of Tula, also known as Tollan Xicocolitlan, a Nahuatl phrase that means "near the cattails," because it was located near three continuously flowing rivers, the largest of which is the Tula River. Tula was considered rather independent, even though its location was within the northern edge of the Aztec Empire.

Some of the objects within the museum were large sculptured figures of warriors. "Look at this one," I said. "It depicts a warrior in quilted armor with arms held above his head."

Maya explained that the figure with raised arms is one of many that once supported an altar. "The warrior figure embodies the mingling of warfare and religion, a significant emphasis at Tula."

The Tula site includes the Ceremonial Center of the Tula Grande - an area called "Tula Chico," the Guadalupe Mastoche Center, which contains two pyramids with Atlas figures, two main ballcourts, and other large buildings, one with a series of columns that faced a large plaza. The central plaza is large enough to hold 100,000 people.

The major attraction at Tula is Pyramid B, also known as Pyramid Quetzalcoatl or Morning Star. It is a five-tiered structure with massive columns on top. Maya said that each column is the likeness of a Toltec warrior.

"Each of the warrior column is fifteen feet tall, and each carries an atlatl or spear thrower and wears a butterfly chest plate in front and a backside plate in the shape of a solar disk. Notice that all the walls are adorned with sculptured snakes."

Johnathan, reading the brochure, said, "Tula fell around 1150, but had significant influence in the Aztec Empire. In fact, the feathered serpent god Quetzalcoatl is first identified with Tula, not with the Aztecs."

Although we did not pay much attention to the surroundings at first, but with Tula rivers and streams on all sides, and our attention shifted to the birdlife. That change was largely due a vermilion flycatcher that Maya saw. "Look at that gorgeous little red bird. What is it?" With her question, we began to look about and saw the flycatcher and a number of other species.

Another bird along the edge of the compound was a curve-billed thrasher. I had heard its very distinct calls, like an emphatic "whit whuit," a number of times, but it finally dawned on me what it was when I found one along the edge of the clearing. Other species that we saw within the compound included numerous great-tailed grackles, a number of bronzed cowbirds, and a blue grosbeak.

When we walked along the river, I saw a rufous-backed robin. "Johnathan, there is a rufous-backed robin, ahead of us in the tree. That is a lifer for me." In another couple minutes, I said, "There in the river are some Mexican ducks."

"They look like mallards to me. What is the difference?" Johnathan asked.

"Mallards don't occur this far south, and these birds lack the distinct green head of male mallards. Mexican ducks do mate with mallards, however, so when found in the southern U.S., they are always suspect."

Chloe and Maya had lingered behind, and when I looked for them, they were standing behind us on the riverbank. "Come over here," Maya said. "I have found a tiny little bird. I think it is a kingfisher. But it is much smaller than those I see back home."

"That, my dear friend, is a green kingfisher," I said. Just then it flew from its perch and dove head first into the river. In another second or two, it flew out of the water with a fish held tightly in its bill, it returned to its perch, flipped the fish up, and swallowed it head-first.

"After watching that kingfisher, I can understand why you two are interested in birds," Maya said. "Maybe I will become a bird-watcher."

The bird of the day, however, was a peregrine falcon. "Look!" I shouted, "There is a falcon! It's a peregrine. Check it's facial pattern and long pointed wings."

It flew down the river and out of sight

"Are you sure," Johnathan asked.

"Yes, I had a good look at it, and I could clearly see the black cheek wedge and striped belly. That is one unbelievable bird!"

Chloe asked, "Is a peregrine special? Why are you so excited?"

"Indeed, it is. The peregrine is considered the fastest bird in the world, and it is one of the few birds that occur world-wide. Peregrines are able to prey on fast flying birds and even bats. They are masters of the air."

Before long we were back among the ruins. It was obvious to me that our enthusiasm for more ruins had reached a low point. I would have spent more time looking for birds, but my companions, maybe because the afternoon was quite warm and humid, were ready to return to town and get ready for dinner.

CHAPTER 17

MEXICO CITY, TEXCOCO

THE FOUR OF us – Maya, Chloe and Johnathan and I – met for breakfast the next morning, and after ordering, I asked a number of questions about the early history of Mexico. Before going to sleep last night, I had made a long list in my mind; now I was eager to get some answers.

"Maya," I said, "Johnathan and I have visited numerous ruins during the last few weeks, from the Yucatan to Tula, and, although I know that those on the Yucatan were Mayan, I now come face to face with Toltec and Aztec ruins; help me to understand the different cultures and time-periods."

"That is a big order, but I will try to provide you with some perspective of the early peoples as best I can. First, let me say that much of what is now known is based on archeological evidence uncovered only since the first decades of the twentieth century. Even today, there isn't complete agreement on many of the stages of development. However, almost everyone agrees that the earliest presence of man in Mexico began about 1800 B.C. Those people were hunter-gatherers who had no permanent residence. But when those same people discovered corn, or maize, they became farmers who occupied a permanent place."

"That is pretty much the same history as the native peoples in the United States. But when did they begin to build the great pyramids and palaces that we find today?"

"Keep in mind that the various peoples, such as the Olmec, Zapotec, Toltec, Mayan, and Aztec, occupied different geographic areas of the country. The Olmec people, the most ancient civilization, probably arose about 1400 B.C. The Zapotec civilization arose sometime before 400 B.C. Their greatest achievement was the construction of Monte Alban. The Toltec people settled in the Valley earlier than the Aztecs."

"You mentioned geographical areas of the country. I understand that the Mayans occupied most of the Yucatan, but where did the earlier Olmecs live?"

"The Olmec heartland was along the Gulf Coast, from what is now called Alvarado south to the Rio Tonelli and included the Tuxtla Mountains."

"We spent time in the Catemaco area, primarily looking at birds, but didn't realize the significance of the area relating to the ancient Olmecs. Did the Olmecs build temples and palaces like the Mayans," I asked.

"They didn't build large structures like the Mayans, but they did build ceremonial centers. Their structures were rarely more than two or three stories in height. One of the Olmec's principal characteristics was their carving ability. Excavations of all the known Olmec sites have uncovered an abundance of stone figures, many of which are so well done that you can identify detailed characteristics. For instance, I have seen a basalt figure of a women with a baby in her arms, and another figure of a bearded man in a wrestling position. And I also have seen an Olmec wooden mask, encrusted with jade."

"Where have you seen those relicts you mentioned, "I asked.

"Most are located in Mexico City, at the National Museum, but others are located in local museums at the ruins themselves. If you have the opportunity to visit the museum in Mexico City, do so. Some of the relicts on display are amazing. For instance, there is a huge, carved, round head of a ruler with a helmet-like headgear. And there are many smaller carved figures; some are carved out of jade."

"Are there some artifacts from Tula there, too," Johnathan asked.

"Yes, I remember two. One is a large carving that depicts the birth of King Topiltzin that emphasizes his association with the Plumed Serpent Quetzalcóatl. Another is a ceramic Tlaloc that emphasizes that god's curling snake 'moustache.'"

"Were moustaches in at that time?" I asked.

"No, the majority of ceramic heads I have seen from that time were hairless."

"The Olmec Empire and civilization were the dominate culture from as early as 1500 B.C. to at least to 400 B.C. But even earlier, they had built the highland settlement of Chalcatzingo. The Olmecs had a lasting influence, especially in religious practices. In fact, the Olmecs developed the religious rites involving human sacrifices and blood-letting."

"What could possibly be the purpose for such practices?"

Maya answered, "All of those early cultures were steeped in religious rites, and the priests held the upper hand when it came to such behavior. The priests believed in sacrifices to appease their gods. In most cases, captured soldiers were used, but there were cases when a priest sent his helpers out to round up non-soldiers for sacrificing."

"The Toltecs must have been a blood-thirsty lot. Did the Zapotecs and other cultures that arose afterwards follow some of the same behavior," I asked.

"I must admit that most did, right up to and including the Aztecs."

"Our guidebook states that the city of Tula was destroyed by Chichimec tribesman in 1150," Johnathan said. "Who were the Chichimec people? I don't remember hearing about the Chichimec before now."

"The Chichimec were nomadic tribes from northwestern Mexico. Father Sahagun wrote that they were 'wild' people who lived in caves and clothed themselves in animal skins and yucca-fiber sandals. It is written that it was the Chichimec god, Hultzilopochtli, who gave those early wanderers the new name, Mexica. Not until the 19th century were they called Azteca."

"It is hard to believe that those early Toltecs changed so drastically from hunter-gathers to builders of great platforms, and then so much of their structures were destroyed by Chichimec nomads," I said.

I spent a few minutes thinking about all of that, and then asked, "You said that Monte Alban was constructed by the Zapotecs. I remember from our visit to Monte Alban that the Zapotec civilization lasted until the fall of the Aztec Empire. Did the Monte Alban civilization extend beyond the Oaxaca Valley?"

"The Zapotecs built several cities in the central highlands. The best known of those is Teotihuacan, which was built at about the same time as the birth of Jesus. Teotihuacan became important as a trading center because of its location, along the San Juan River, was close to obsidian deposits that so many of the people used in weapon-making."

"It appears that Teotihuacan and Monte Alban flourished at the same time," I said. "Can I assume that Teotihuacan, because of its proximity to Tenochtitlán, became a member of the Aztec Empire?"

"Yes. When the Aztecs built Tenochtitán, they copied many features from Teotihuacan. Also, according to Aztec writings, they were greatly impressed by Teotihuacan."

Later that evening, I lay in bed trying to place all the ruins in some sort of order. Within a few days, we were going to be in the Aztec capitol of Tenochtitán, and I wanted to put all the ruins we had visited, as well as those that we had not seen, in perspective. Our visits to ruins had not been organized; we saw some of the later ones first and some of the earlier ones last. But I tried nevertheless.

My attempt started out pretty well. The Monte Alban ruins were the oldest, Teotihuacan was next, then El Tajín and Mazapan soon afterward, and then Tenochtitán. But where do the Mayans fit? I remembered reading at one of the Mayan ruins that the 'classic' Mayan period occurred from about 250 to 900. That would mean that the Mayan civilization occurred during the mid-period of the Zapotec period, the same time frame as the building of Monte Alban, and about the same time that the Toltecs built Mazapan, about 500 years before the Aztec Empire arose. I felt kind of proud of myself at the time, but as I drifted off to sleep, I also realized that my time-table for the various ruins was pretty wobbly.

At breakfast the next morning, as I recited my thinking from the previous night, I was met with both admiration and skepticism by Maya. After we had finished breakfast, Maya said, "Robert, your time-table was accurate in a very general way, but you ignored some of the other major civilizations. For example, Zacatenco in the central highlands, La Venta in the southern Gulf Coast region, and Remojadas in the northern central gulf region all began at about the turn of the first century."

"Maya, I truly admire your knowledge of that early history. I guess, unless I decide to become a scholar of early Mexico history, I will be satisfied with the history of the ruins I have visited. But thank you for helping me better understand a time table for their construction and inhabitants."

After a few minutes, I said, "Maya, you know that Johnathan and I are going to Mexico City today. We plan to spend time at the Tenochtitlan ruins, but do you have some advice for us about visiting any other sites? We have a few more days in Mexico before we will need to go home."

"It's been several years since I spent any time within the Mexico City region, and that was before I decided to study Mexico history. Maybe that was what triggered my initial interest. I have one suggestion. Of all the cities in the greater Mexico City region, I enjoyed Texcoco most of all. That city, with its many gardens, is a favorite."

Before going to bed, Johnathan and I studied the maps in our guidebook, and by bedtime, we had a plan for the next few days.

After breakfast, Johnathan and I said our farewell to Chloe and Maya; they planned to spend another day in Tula de Allende. Johnathan and I headed south toward the big city, but instead of going directly into the center of the Mexico City, we stayed to the east and arrived in Texcoco by mid-afternoon. After driving around the city, we got a room at the Hotel Posada Santa Bertha.

When checking in, Johnathan asked the clerk about where to find the central plaza and a good restaurant. The clerk, José Morales, immediately said that the best restaurant in the entire city was right there at the hotel; he seemed a little peeved that we did not already known about its reputation. He also told us that the central plaza was about two blocks away. After finding our room, we walked over to the plaza. It was similar to most of the other plazas in Mexico, a large open area with numerous trees and several small gardens with walkways that crossed the center and along the edge where there were a number of benches. We decided to sit for awhile before returning to the hotel for dinner.

The people at the plaza were not the fun-loving, joyous people that we had found at Tula de Allende. Maybe it is because Texcoco was so close to the big city, but the majority of the people seemed more serious. It was not what I had expected for a city that was known for its gardens and flowers.

We had chosen a bench with a view of two of the garden plots, both containing an abundance of flowering plants.

After a short time, the two gardens seemed to come alive.

"Robert, there is a hummingbird to the right."

I immediately found it in my binoculars, and in another couple minutes, I called out, "It's a broad-billed hummingbird! Look at its all green back and bright red bill. That is one super bird, and it is a lifer for me."

It didn't stay long, but we stayed on our bench thinking that maybe another hummingbird might appear. Sure enough, in about ten minutes, we found a second hummingbird. This one also had a red bill, but its sides and tail were a cinnamon color.

"That my friend is a berylline hummingbird; another lifer," I said.

As if on cue, a large flock of parrots flew overhead, heading to a nighttime roost.

"I think they are red-lored parrots," I said. "I can see their yellow eye-rings and red forehead."

"That was a good-sized flock. How many were there," Johnathan asked.

"At least 20, but maybe more."

Just after I said that, a flock of parakeets flew by.

"What are those" Johnathan asked.

"I think they are green parakeets, but I also saw some other species in that flock. My guess is that other, maybe non-natives, have joined up with the native species."

Almost as might be expected, a large number of cattle egrets flew past our viewing area, going in the same direction as the parrots and parakeets. The egrets were stretched out in long lines, some in a V-pattern, and a few loners as well. "You can bet the egrets have been feeding in a field nearby and are heading to their roost, probably along the lake."

We ate that evening at the hotel and afterwards walked back to the plaza, where we again sat on a bench and watched the people. We were approached by a young man, probably still in his teens, who asked us where in the United States we were from. For some reason, I had an instant dislike for him. He looked kind of rugged and he wore a headscarf and was covered with tattoos, plus he was smoking a cigarette. Even before we could answer his questions, he began to explain that he was lost in Mexico City without any money. He asked if we could possible give him a few dollars so he could eat. He said, "I have not eaten for three days, and you would be blessed if you helped a fellow American."

Although neither Johnathan or I had been around many dopers, we seemed to react exactly the same negative way. Johnathan told him: "No. We do not have any extra money, so please go away."

I guess Johnathan's answer surprised him. He stared at us a minute, and flipped us off and walked away. "That was a pleasant fellow. With an attitude like that, he may never eat! I noticed, however, that he had enough money to buy cigarettes, but not enough to eat."

The next morning found us at the ruins of Texcoco, also known as Alteptl, which was located along the eastern bank of Lake Texcoco, northeast of downtown Mexico City. We purchased a brochure with our entry tickets and were immediately immersed within a colorful scene. The site managers had tried to maintain much of the same image as before the Conquest. Johnathan, reading in the brochure, said, "At the time of the Conquest, Texcoco was one of the largest and most prestigious cities in Central Mexico, with a population about 24,000 inhabitants. It was second only to Tenochtitlan. Texcoco was founded by Xolotl in 1115, and he reigned until 1232. Xolotl was followed by ten rulers after his death. The sixth ruler, Netzahualcoyotl, was best known as a poet, a patron of the arts, and a philosopher."

From anywhere in the compound, the "Royal Residence" was visible on a hill known as Texcotingo.

"That is one huge structure," I said.

"Indeed. According to the brochure, it had three hundred chambers, as well as its own aqueduct, baths, stairwells and gardens. The gardens, prior to the Conquest, had a vast collection of plants from all over the Aztec Empire."

Johnathan continued, "The whole hill was watered by a canal system he constructed. He designed it as a sacred place to honor the rain god, Tlaloc. At the very top he constructed a shrine to Tlaloc, with 520 marble steps. That is a significant number, since, according to Aztec mythology, the gods had the choice to destroy humanity once every 52 years."

"Did they get water from the lake, and if so, they must have had some method a transferring it up-hill to the residence."

"No," Johnathan said. "The water used to irrigate the gardens was derived from the mountains by canals carved into the rock. And get this, Netzahualcoyotl built in waterfalls. The route of the canals crossed a deep canyon that ran from north to south. So, he had it filled with tons of rocks, stones and dirt. That effort resulted in one of the earliest aqueducts in the New World."

"That man must have been a genius," I said.

"What's more, "Johnathan added, "His hill-top residence was considered a 'center of learning;' it had a famous library that included books from older Mesoamerican civilizations."

"So, was all of that destroyed by Cortez?"

"No, although much of the area had been rebuilt by the time of the Conquest, much of the original materials had been looted and destroyed by the Chichimec, who then claimed the area for themselves. They were expelled about 1337 by the Acolhua peoples with Tepanee help. From 1827 to 1830, Texcoco was the capitol of the state of Mexico."

By the time we got back to the hotel it was dark. Instead of leaving the hotel to find another restaurant, we ate right there, at the Hotel Posada Santa Bertha, and we were glad we did. Our meals were marvelous, and the waitress, Carla Hernández, was excellent, and we spent far more time with our dinner than we normally would.

"Robert, I think I will ask Carla if she will marry me. Would you be my best man?" Johnathan joked.

"Johnathan, we have so far got along extremely well, but that may soon come to an end. I was planning to marry Carla."

Eventually, we returned to our room, and I was soon asleep and dreaming about Carla.

At breakfast the next morning, Carla was not in sight. Instead, our waitress was a much older women, but she seemed to be as capable as Carla, although she lacked certain features that Carla had possessed.

"Johnathan," I said. "I am not looking forward to driving in Mexico City. The traffic, I hear, is horrible. So, I have a suggestion. First, let's find out where the airport is located, and we can drive that far, get a room nearby, and we can take taxis to where we want to go in the city."

"That sounds like a great idea to me. I have been told there is a Holiday Inn very near the entrance to the airport, and we can stay there."

"I like that." Our map provided all the information we needed to find our way. In spite of the traffic, by noontime, we reach the Holiday Inn and secured a room.

CHAPTER 18

MEXICO CITY, THE NATIONAL MUSEUM OF ANTHROPOLOGY

OUR PLAN TO stay at the Mexico City Holiday Inn was a good one. Although it was not much different than other Holiday Inns, it gave us access to the airport and a place we could call home while visiting various sites in and around the city.

By the time we checked in and found our room, it was lunchtime. We first spent a few minutes studying our guidebook map in order to get an idea of what areas we wanted to visit. Our most important destination, of course, was the ruins of Tenochtitlan, but we knew we also wanted to see the National Museum. We found ourselves unsure which of the two sites should be first. It made good sense to spend time in the museum, and then go to the ruins, but the opposite plan also made good sense.

With that issue unsettled, we decided to have lunch in the hotel restaurant. In the hotel lobby, we saw a travel office off the lobby that we had not noticed earlier. We entered to find a lady who was an unusual beauty; olive skin, black eyes and an amazing body. We both just stared at her. Before we could ask a question, she greeted us with a marvelous smile and bright welcoming eyes. "What can I do for you?" she asked. She obviously was Mexican, but she spoke perfect English. It took us almost 20 seconds before we recovered. Before we introduced ourselves and explained our predicament, she introduced herself as Nina Gallardo. Seconds later we were talking about an itinerary for our stay in Mexico City.

"If you have time, I suggest that you first visit the National Museum, then visit Tenochtitlan, and afterwards return again to the museum. I know that you will have questions after visiting the ruins that you can answer with a second visit. You will find some excellent interpreters at the ruins; they can answer any questions you may have. But, I know that seeing the actually relicts and artifacts that are located within the museum will be worthy of your time." We talked about those options during lunch and decided to follow her recommendations. Just after that decision, a young lady approached us and said: "Buenos días, seniors. Nina, in the travel office, told me that you are asking questions about an itinerary for your visit to Mexico City. I am a registered guide, and if you are interested, I would welcome the opportunity to assist you. My name is Katrina Luzón; I am a resident of Mexico City, and I have been taught all about our ruins and our museums."

I asked, "What do you charge? Is it an hourly or a daily rate?"

"Either way you would prefer," she answered. "And a second day's charge would be only an additional half of one day. If you wish for me to drive you in my own car, that charge would be an additional twenty dollars each day."

"Katrina, please give us a few minutes to talk about your offer. We will meet you in the lobby after we finish our meal," I said.

When she left, I said, "I think that Katrina's offer would be well worth the price."

"Besides," Johnathan added, "Katrina is one lovely lady. Maybe she has a sister."

So, with little more discussion, we told Katrina that we agreed with her offer. We returned to our room to pick up our packs and met Katrina in the lobby. She asked us where we wanted to go first. "Which one would you recommend, Tenochtitlan or the National Museum?" I asked.

"Let me take you to the museum first. Then, depending upon how much time you take there, we can go to the ruins. However, I think you will want to spend a whole day at Tenochtitlan; we can do that tomorrow."

"OK, let's go to the museum first," Johnathan said.

"I agree."

And with that we were off to the National Museum of Anthropology.

Katrina almost immediately began a discussion about the Aztecs. "How much do you know about the Aztecs?" she asked

Johnathan responded that he had read a lot about Mexico history, and I added: "We have just finished a lengthy tour of ruins on the Yucatan, where we visited many of the Mayan sites, and we also spent time at Olmec and Toltec sites, but we are now anxious to see Tenochtitlan."

"You will see that Tenochtitlan is the grandest of them all. The Aztec Empire, that arose about 1300, was at its peak at the time of the Conquest. It contained a number of ethnic groups, but they all spoke Nahuatl. By 1427, the Aztec culture was organized into city-states, some of which joined to form alliances or political confederations."

"What was the extent of the Aztec Empire at its height?" I asked.

"The Aztec Empire was a compilation of peoples throughout central Mexico. From the 14th through the 16th centuries, they called themselves Mexicah; that is where the name of Mexico was derived. The capital of the Aztec Empire was Tenochtitlan, which was built on raised islands in Lake Texcoco. The Mexico City we know today was constructed much later on some portions of the ruins of Tenochtitlan."

"Is it true that the city is slowly sinking?" I asked.

"Yes," she answered. "It was built on what was a lake, and our geologists assert that is the case."

By then, we had arrived at the museum. Katrina let us off at the entrance, and she drove off to find a parking space. She said she would meet us inside; she also told us she had free access so we did not need to buy her a ticket.

The very sight of the enormous structure surprised me. Johnathan said, "This is amazing. I have dreamed for years about visiting this museum. You know that my father had seen it many years ago, when he was a history major at the University of Florida. I have heard many stories about its wonderful contents. And now I am to see it for myself."

Before entering, we stood out in front for a several minutes, trying to absorb the general scene. It stands on several acres of parkland with the slopes of Chapultepec rising above it like the setting of one of the ancient ruins.

Just inside was the Museum's Mexica Hall. We stopped to gaze at the Stone of the Fifth Sun, a 26-ton basalt disk. An interpretive sign explained that its iconography records the Aztec's view of the cosmos and predicts their doom with the inevitable waning of the Fifth Son.

Katrina had, by now, caught up with us. "The Aztecs were pessimistic people; read the carving on the adjacent wall." I read aloud: "Will I leave only this: Like the flowers that whither? Will nothing last in my name?"

Looming over the Mexica Hall was a huge stone relief that is known as "She of the Serpent Skirt." It presents an image that is both horrific and oddly compelling. As we stared at it, Katrina said, "That relief was discovered in a 1790 excavation near the Templo Mayor. The Dominicans reburied it because of the fear that it produced, especially in children."

I could understand that. The figure sprouted a pair of serpent heads and it wore a necklace of human hands and hearts.

Katrína added, "Such details represent Aztec concepts of procreativeness as well as death."

Next was a huge figure that included sculptured creatures and a human head, all emerging from a tortoise shell. "That is the head of Macuilxochilt, god of music. Aztec sculpture often blends the earthly with the divine. One scholar stated that it represented what is found, like man, between sky and soil, in the mortal realm of life and death."

"Katrina, you seem to know much about what we are seeing in this museum; how many times have you visited the museum?"

"I don't know. I first visited the museum when I was a little girl. My father worked here as a guide for many years, and I accompanied him on many occasions. He passed away two years ago, and I have many fond memories of him each time I visit the museum, especially the Mexica Hall where he spent most of his time."

I said, "I am sorry if I have caused you any sorrow."

"Thank you, but all my memories here are good ones."

As we continued walking the halls of the museum, we encountered hundreds of relicts, large and small, and many reminded us of some of the ruins we had visited.

"Robert, come look at this. It is the stone jaguar from Tula that held hearts of sacrificial victims; notice its hollow back."

A minute later, Johnathan said, "Here is the greenstone sculpture of a snake from Texcoco."

Next was the "Stone of Tizoc." We stopped to admire its fascinating sculptures that covered the entire top and sides of the huge stone. When Katrina saw us looking at it, she said "That is the Stone of Tizoc; it was unearthed in 1791 by workers at the Zocalo. Its carvings are said to record the expansion of the empire under Tizoc, seventh ruler of Tenochtitlan. It depicts Mexica lords gripping the hair of foreign deities, who are bending forward submissively. It includes fifteen scenes depicting the conquest of Tizoc. It also is written that Tizoc was a weak ruler and a poor general, so someone poisoned him."

"Those early Aztecs apparently demanded much from their leaders."

As we continued to wander about the museum, I said, "Johnathan, look at this." I was staring at a huge round shield covered with reddish feathers and inside was a bizarre dragon-like creature of turquoise stones, rimmed in gold.

"That center figure is said to represent a coyote that is emitting a device that combines water and fire. It is an Aztec metaphor for war," Katrina said.

Next to the shield were a number of weapons that were used by the Aztecs. Most impressive was a sword-club with side grooves set with razor-sharp obsidian blades. There, too, were spears with sharp, barbed blades, and darts that could be hurled from an atlatl.

"Robert, check this out," Johnathan said. He was looking at a fascinating weapon, a 39-inch-long sawfish blade. The description read that it was found at the bottom of a stone box packed with thousands of other ceremonial objects at the Templo Mayor.

Katrina then said: "Archeologists have found a total of seventy-seven sawfish blades, and this one is the longest. The Aztec believed that sawfish had deep spiritual significance because the fish were considered a hybrid of earth and sea."

An additional nearby sign read, "The sawfish blade, with its sharpest teeth intact, was the last object to be excavated from the deposit containing some 11,800 artifacts, including the carcass of a wolf dressed in gold armor, birds, and thousands of snails. The box was interred under a floor during the reign of emperor Ahuitzotl (1486-1502) and may be a tribute to the expansion of the Aztec realm under his rule."

Also, nearby was a plaque that provided an expression of Aztec philosophy. I read it out loud. "The battlefield is the place

> Where one toasts the divine liquor in war.
> Where are stained red the divine eagles,
> Where the jaguars howl,
> Where all kinds of precious stone rain from ornaments,
> Where wave headdresses rich with fine plumes,
> Where princes are smashed to bits."

"That is one fascinating tribute to war and death. But I am curious," I said. "What is the divine liquor in war?"

"Oh, yes," Katrina responded. "Pulque was considered to be the drink of the gods. It has been included in ancient writings as early as 9,000 years ago. It was derived from mysticism. It was considered a gift of the goddess Mayahuel, who was connected to the moon, and was the godess of fertility and nutrition. Plus, the more one drank, the further the spirit was able to travel from the body."

"Although I never drank pulque, I have a good imagination," I said. "I love a good Margarita, and I assume, since both are products of agave plants, drinking pulque works just as well."

Johnathan said, "One of my uncles, who lives in the Florida Panhandle, made his own tequila. He had his own garden of agaves. The problem for him was that agaves take twelve to fourteen years before they are ready."

"That's a long wait. But once it is an adult plant, what steps did he take to make his own tequila?" Katrina asked. "Agaves send up a stalk that can reach twenty feet high, and they die after blooming. The stalk is cut down, and a deep bowl is cut out of the center. That bowl soon fills with the natural juices of the agave, up to a quarter of a gallon several times for up to one year. Although I have not personally seen this done, those juices are scooped out and let ferment. That is pulque."

"How is that different from tequila?" I asked

"When fermentation occurs, you can drink that, pulque, but when those same juices are distilled, that is tequila. I am told that there are lots of brands of tequila. It has become a major industry in the United States," Johnathan answered.

"It is said that the Aztec priests declared pulque a privilege that was limited only to the priestly culture, and that may have been a major reason for the people to lose respect for them," Katrina said.

We continued to wander though the museum. "Robert, take a look at this flint knife," Johnathan said. It was a sacrificial knife. The blade was carved from flint with a mosaic-incrusted handle in the form of an Eagle Knight. "You must admit that the Aztecs had some excellent workmen; that handle is exquisite," he added.

The obsidian mirror was perhaps the most fascinating of all the artifacts we saw.

"I can't believe that the Aztecs were able to cut obsidian so thin as to make a mirror," I said.

Katrina added, "The obsidian mirror was sacred to Tezcatlipoca, god of shamans. It is one the many objects that Cortez sent to Spain."

Everywhere we turned we saw fascinating relicts, and we were so engrossed in what we were seeing that we didn't realized it was late afternoon. We had not eaten anything since breakfast, and we were starving.

"Katrina," I said, "We are enjoying the museum immensely, but we are hungry. How about taking you out for dinner at one of your favorite restaurants?"

"I would truly appreciate that, but I am meeting my girlfriend for dinner. I must beg off."

"In that case, how about us taking you and your girlfriend out for dinner? We would be honored to do so."

She thought for a few seconds and then said, "Yes, I would like that. I can call Jerri, and she can meet us there. Are you sure? I do not want to impose."

"You are not imposing at all. We would like to meet your girlfriend, and we can be two couples."

The restaurant, the Mariposa Bonita, was lovely. A butterfly motif dominated the rooms, and it contained smaller, more intimate sections that had an air of sensuality. I was unsure whether it was only my imagination or whether my instincts were correct. We were shown to a closed room and were soon ordering a cocktail or wine while we waited for Katrina's girlfriend. Jerri was a beautiful young lady who fit right in to the established mood. Plus, she had a body that could only be described as voluptuous. It was obvious, at least to me, that Katrina had a strong feeling for Johnathan; I had noticed that closeness all though the day. I assumed that Katrina had invited Jerri to join us as a partner for me. I was not one to argue.

After our pre-dinner drinks arrived, we gave a toast to a good and productive day. I asked Jerri where she worked. "Yes. I am a legal secretary. I work in a lawyer's office on the outer edge of the city. That is why it took me considerable to time to get to the Mariposa; it is my all-time favorite place to eat. When Katrina called, I could not refuse."

We continued talking about our activities that day, as well as some of our earlier stops.

"How long do you plan to spend in Mexico City?" she asked.

"We are unsure, but we hope to see the more of the museum and also the ruins."

When she asked if we had had a good day so far, we both immediately expressed our pleasure. "We could not have had a better day. We so appreciate Katrina's knowledge of the museum; she was a perfect host!" I exclaimed.

"What are your plans for tomorrow? Are you going to see Tenochtitlan?"

"Yes, we are; that is the purpose of coming to Mexico City," I said. "But I admit that the museum is the frosting on the cake."

Both grinned at my comment, and Katrina said, "Robert, we have not heard that expression before, but it fits very well."

Dinner that evening, after several drinks, was superb. We lingered long after dinner, until the manager seemed to encourage us to leave. The restaurant was getting very busy by about 11 pm.

Leaving the restaurant, we stood at Katrina's car for a considerable time; it was if none of us wanted to leave. Finally, it was Johnathan who said, "It is getting very late, and we have a full day ahead of us."

I said to Katrina, "If we eat here again tomorrow night, I would love for Jerri to join us. Is that alright with you, Jerri?"

"Yes, I would like that. I would love to hear about your day at the ruins." She turned to me and said, "Robert, I would like to know more about you and any details you care to share about your life in America. Someday I plan to go to America. It has long been a dream of my lifetime."

"I would love to tell you about America and my life on St. Croix in the Virgin Islands."

We left the restaurant, with Katrina driving us back to the Holiday Inn. En route, she said, "Robert, you have an admirer in Jerri. Jerri has been hurt recently by a man she planned to marry, and so she is very vulnerable."

"I am sorry to hear that. I have no plans to hurt her. She seems to be a really sweet person. If she joins us again for dinner this evening, I will be very careful. I didn't know that she was grieving."

"I trust you Robert. I am telling you this so you will be gentle."

"Thank you for your trust in telling me about her. And now, as late as it is after that superb dinner, it's time for me to get some sleep. What time should we be ready in the morning?"

"I will meet you in the restaurant at 9 am. Good night Robert and Johnathan. Sweet dreams."

Back in our room, we talked briefly about Katrina's comments about Jerri. I certainly had no intention of doing anything that would hurt her. By then, I realized that my thoughts were pretty well centered around Carol. We changed the conversation to what a marvelous day we had experienced at the museum and our dinner at the Mariposa. Very soon I was fast asleep.

CHAPTER 19

TENOCHTITLAN

K ATRINA MET US at the restaurant the following morning. She greeted us with: "I hope you two had a good night. Jerri told me to tell you that she will meet us again tonight for dinner. We can leave for Tenochtitlan as soon as you are ready."

After returning to our room and gathering our packs, we met Katrina in the lobby and were soon off to Tenochtitlan. Since it was all the way across the city, it took us considerable time. En route we were able to ask a number of questions. "I am told that Moctezuma welcomed Cortez at first. Why was he so naive to accept the Spaniards?"

"Moctezuma believed that the arrival of the Spaniards was linked to the supposed return of an exiled god, Quetzalcoatl, who was to return as a 'pale and bearded' human. When he learned that the Spaniards had arrived by sea on a 'small mountain that moved, floating in the midst of the water,' it verified his belief of a returning god.

"Moctezuma so accepted their arrival that he actually sent an envoy to the coast to present Cortez with exotic gifts. Those including a serpent mask of precious stones and a cape made from quetzal feathers. In return for the gifts, Cortez gave the emissaries glass beads, trinkets and food. He also demonstrated his cannons. When those emissaries told Moctezuma about the cannons and their lethal fire power, he became deeply depressed.

"He was told that the cannons were able to "throw a ball of stone out of its entrails, shooting sparks and raining fire. The smoke that comes out with it has a pestilent odor, like that of rotten mud… If the cannon is aimed against a mountain, the mountain splits and cracks open.

"Moctezuma, of course, knew nothing of the Spaniards, but it was the year One Reed in the Aztec calendar, an anniversary of Quetzalcoatl's mythical birth and a suitable year for his return."

"But, what was the reason that Cortez was along the coast in the first place?" I asked.

"He was searching for members of an earlier expedition that had been shipwrecked on the Yucatan coast. He and his soldiers went ashore to search for the lost sailors, as well to trade with the local inhabitants. While in the Yucatan, he captured numerous Mayans, including Dona Marina, who became his concubine, translator, and adviser during his time in the New World. Cortez commanded eleven ships that carried more than 300 soldiers, a few cannons, and sixteen horses. In those days, it was a powerful force!"

"Was Cortez peaceful at first? What was it that created such a change?" I asked.

"Historians believe that the change occurred when he received the spectacular gifts from Moctezuma. When Cortez realized that many of the gifts were precious stones, he decided he wanted more. When he later met Moctezuma, Cortez found him dressed in truly regal clothing.

"I am told that the captured Mayans and Toltecs were used as guides and bearers, and that his army created havoc along the way to meet Moctezuma in Tenochtitlan.

"Word about the potential danger got out fast. I read somewhere that when he reached the first inland village of Totanacs, one of the cities on the eastern edge of the Aztec Empire, it was deserted."

"I can only imagine what Cortez thought at the first sight of Tenochtitlan. It must have been a huge surprise," I said.

Tenochtitlan was a vast metropolis built on a raised island on Lake Texcoco. It had four causeways that extended out from the city center. In 1519, it was at the height of its glory with as many as 300,000 inhabitants. It was the center of a vast empire of Nahuati-speaking peoples that as early as 1427 had been organized into city-states, some of which joined to form alliances or political confederations.

There is a written description of Tenochtitlan by Bernal Diaz del Castillo, one of Cortez's soldiers, that describes his first impression on seeing the Aztec citadel:

> During the morning, we arrived at a broad causeway and continued our march towards Iztapalapa [Tenochtitlan], and when we saw so many cities and villages built in the water and other great towns on dry land and that straight and level causeway going towards Mexico, we were amazed and said that it was like the enchantments they tell of in the legend of Amalis, on account of the great towers and temples and buildings rising from the water, and all built of masonry. And some of our soldiers asked whether the things that we saw were not a dream.

"I'm assuming that Montezuma realized fairly soon that the Spaniards were not there for peaceful purposes" I said.

"Indeed. The Spaniards soon began to loot the city. When they discovered the various 'devil practices' of the Aztecs, such as sacrificing their enemies and others, the Christians could not tolerate such behavior."

"Keep in mind that the Aztecs believed that it was their duty to 'feed the gods' with human sacrifices. The Florentine Codex contained a statement that "blood nourishes the deities, thus sustaining the world'.

"Conquest of the city and all of the Aztec Empire began almost immediately. Although the military might of the Aztecs, that was superior to all its neighbors, was no match to that of the Spaniards, who had cannons and other more modern weapons, as well as horses. In addition to direct combat, siege and psychological warfare, diseases such as smallpox, which was brought to the New World by the Spaniards, took their toll.

"In one early battle for Tenochtitlan, however, the Spaniards were overcome by sheer numbers of Aztec fighters, and in retreating from the city, they suffered strategic losses. That loss thereafter became known as the *La Noches Tristes* or Night of Sorrow.

"In addition," Katrina said, "the Aztecs took captives during the battles and they were sacrificed. Their heads, as well as horse heads, were mounted on spikes. This created even greater hatred by the Spaniards.

"Gradually, the mighty Aztec Empire came under Spanish control. The last of the tributary states, Cuauhtémoc, surrendered on August 13, 1521. But it took another 60 years before the war between the Spaniards and the Aztecs was concluded, and it took almost 170 years more before Spain's conquest of the Yucatan was completed.

"Following the fall of Tenochtitlan, Montezuma was led away in chains, and Cortez proclaimed all the 'land and its soil' for Spain."

My first impression of Tenochtitlan was of a great open area dotted with numerous structures, some of which are huge. The Great Temple of Tlaloc and Huitzilopochtli dominates the entire compound. Behind it was the Temple of Tezcatlipoca, and to the left was the smaller Temple of Colhuacan.

"Before we walk through the grounds, let's visit the museum. They have a panorama that provides an excellent perspective of the entire central area," Katrina said.

We entered the museum, where we paid a small fee, purchased a brochure, and then stood in front of the panorama which did indeed provide us with a marvelous perspective of the major portion of Tenochtitlan.

"The Spaniards razed the city, but much later, by consulting old documents, architects created this model. I think they did a wonderful job. You can see the symmetry and order of the ancient city," Katrina said

Indeed, we could. For me, that panorama added an understanding of Aztec organization and precision.

The stop at the museum was a good and valuable step before entering the compound. One of the first structures I noticed was a round temple. It was very different from the others, and I asked Katrína about its significance.

"That is a five-tiered temple to honor Quetzalcoatl. It was built by Montezuma I between 1440 and 1468, and it was dedicated by the warrior leader Ahuitzotl. That dedication is said to have lasted four days, and according to records, as many as 80,000 victims were sacrificed during the festival. Lines of captives were led to the top of the temple where Ahuitzotl waited, obsidian blade in hand. The sacrificed bodies were flung down the steps that were stained with blood, which the Aztecs understood as the water of life, the sweetest offering to their gods.

"Also notice a dark *tzompantli*, a rack that holds human skulls, alongside."

"Were all those skulls obtained during the festival," I asked,

"Not all. Many of those were from earlier battles with neighboring tribes. I am told that at one time many additional racks held many hundreds of skulls."

While we walked around the compound, I said, "Here is the platform that once held the Stone of Tizoc, the huge carved stone that we saw in the museum yesterday."

Katrina asked, "When we entered the compound, did you notice the wall that surrounds the center area? That wall is known as the Coatepantli or Snake Wall. It encloses the sacred precinct, a paved section of the compound that contains seventy-eight buildings. At one time the stairs to many of those buildings were the sites used to sacrifice victims, and were covered with blood.

"I can't help but wonder how the warriors accepted the fact that they likely would be sacrificed," I said.

"Indeed," Katrina said. "All Aztec warriors accepted that they might die in this way. In fact, it is written that it was a great honor to give their blood for the gods."

"I understand that acts of sacrifice were all part of the Aztec culture, but I can't imagine that there wasn't some dissention. It was a cruel practice," I said. "Not to be too insensitive, but were all or most of the sacrifices done by removing the victim's heart?"

"To the Aztecs, being sacrificed was a great honor, as odd as that seems today. In the Aztec world, it meant they would soon be with the war and sun god, Huitzilopochtli, in his celestial paradise. According to what was written, however, the victim was first ritually bathed and then sacrificed by one of five methods."

"You mean there was actually a personal warrior-victim relationship?" I asked."

"Yes. The victim may have been stretched over a sacrificial stone so the priest could open the chest and cut out the heart with a flint or obsidian knife; the heart was then offered to their god. Or the victim could be decapitated. It is said that decapitation occurred most often with women. A third method was gladiatorial sacrifice."

"That would at least give the victim a chance," Johnathan said.

"Yes and no," Katrina said. "The victim was tethered to a round stone, given an inferior weapon, and then forced to defend himself against a seasoned warrior. Another method was tying the victim to a scaffold and being shot with darts, mainly to provide target practice for young warriors. And still other victims were thrown into a fire time and time again until they died."

"I suppose that those victims, once roasted properly, were then eaten," I joked.

"That is exactly what happened," she said.

Johnathan and I just looked at one another. We didn't comment at the time, but later, when we were alone in our room, the Aztec's methods of sacrifice were a major topic of discussion. It was very obvious that the Aztecs were an extremely blood-thirsty people.

As we continued to wander around the compound, I asked where most of the inhabitants lived.

"At several locations. The large structures that you see on the outer side of the walls were magnificent palaces. That is where the royals lived. But the majority of the population lived far outside the walls, usually in small rock and mud huts."

"Where did Moctezuma live? His palace must have been the highpoint of Tenochtitlan?" I asked.

Johnathan, on checking the brochure, responded, "According to the brochure, his palace was outside the wall, in the far-left corner, next to the House of the Songs."

Katrína said, "Yes. Tenochtitlan contained palaces of several of the rulers, and probably each one had special interests. Those could be music, sports or whatever. Did you notice that the ballcourt was within the wall, very close to the skull rack?"

I tried to make a joke out of that idea, thinking that the next step for the losers at the ballgames might be the skull rack, but I got barely a chuckle.

The more we walked around the compound the more I realized that Tenochtitlan contained many more structures than I originally saw. Looking at the brochure, I found an Eagle House on the Sun Temple, a Temple of Tezcatilpoca, Temple of Colhuacan, the Black House of the Temple of Coatlicue, Palace of Axaycati, Palace of Motecuhzoma Ilhuicamina, Palace of Motecuhzoma Xocoyptzin, and a Royal Aviary.

"What's with a royal aviary," I asked.

"I believe that the Aztecs held captive quetzals. Since feathers of those beautiful birds were used in numerous celebrations and costumes, they must have kept some in captivity."

"I wonder how they were maintained?" I said. "I know that quetzals are fruit-eaters, and I imagine that finding enough food wasn't a problem, but did they keep live birds for any length of time?"

"It could be that other species were kept in the aviary. We have seen several birds in cages along the highways, so I suppose that the Aztecs kept a few songbirds, too. That practice is likely to have originated with the earliest peoples. Certainly, solitaires, tanagers, and euphonias were possible candidates."

Katrina didn't have much to say about birds, but she did say "The Aztecs at Tenochtitlan were well-known traders. They traded for all kinds of things, especially for cotton and fibers. It is logical that colorful birds might have been kept for trading purposes. Before sheep, which were later introduced by the Spaniards, clothing was made from the fibers of the agave plants."

"How much is known about their social activities, such as education, marriage, travels, and other facets of life," I asked.

"A surprising amount. Early writings have mentioned that the city was divided into quadrants, each of which had its own temple, administrative center, principal plaza, and military school with an official that could lead men in wartime. Many Aztec codices that were discovered contained considerable information about their origin. For instance, the first page of Codex Boturini details their long migration across Mexico before founding Tenochtitlan. Other pages of Codex Boturini contains an account of their travels, depicting ancestors leaving their original homeland of Aztlán.

"The Mexica peoples were connected with the Toltecs early-on but they had a falling out in 1323, and their leaders were forced to move on. Those refuges, who began to call themselves Azteca, were barbaric people who dressed in agave fibers. When they arrived in the Valley of Mexico, they killed all the current inhabitants and eventually settled on an island in Lake Texcoco. That settlement became the future home of a glorious empire that would be blessed by the blood-thirsty gods with wealth and fame."

"I have heard that those early people, after leaving Aztlán and searching for a future homesite, looked for an eagle sitting on a cactus that was to mark their homeland. Is that a true story?"

"I am sure that it is. The Codex Mendoza, dating from 1325, illustrates the founding of Tenochtitlan. That Codex contains a wide blue border containing the Aztec calendar and in the center is an eagle sitting on a cactus, and surrounded by ten early Aztec chiefs. Below that is an illustration that depicts the first two conquests of the young Aztec state."

"Tell me about codices. I understand that they contained writings, and that codices were used by both the Mayan and Aztec peoples."

"The Mayan and Aztecs used papyrus, agave fibers, or young animal skins that they had worked into soft paper-like sheets. There are as many as 500 codices available today. The writing was a series of glyphs, either pictorial or alphabetical in form. Codices were used to document all kinds of activities, from major celebrations to daily activities. Although many of the messages have been deciphered, many have not. It is a work that continues."

"It is amazing to me that those early Aztecs were able to construct their city in a lake," I said. "Can you imagine what that would entail?"

Katrina said, "I have read that those settlers first dug canals and piled the cut vegetation up to form mats that were then covered with mud, producing tiny floating islands. They then planted willows and other water-loving plants on those islands. which eventually became large enough and stable enough to build houses on stilts and to grow corn in the fertile soil. The size of that city grew to five square miles."

"But five square miles out of almost nothing is hard to believe."

"It was a slow process, but time was on their side. However, there was another problem for those early settlers, the saltiness of the lake; there were no outlets. King Netzahualcoyotl, the leader at the time, solved that by constructed a ten-mile long dyke to seal off a spring-fed freshwater lagoon. All the land was planted with flowers. It must have been a beautiful city."

"How was the fresh water made available to the city?" I asked.

"The Aztec built aqueducts. Many of those, even today, are still in use."

"There is a Nahuatl poem that suggests that beauty. I think I can remember it." Katrina recited the poem:

> "The city is spread out in circles of jade,
> Radiating flashes of light like quetzal plumes,
> Beside it the lords are borne in boats;
> Over them extends a flowery mist."

"Thank you for that," I said. "The Aztecs were a strange people. They seemed to appreciate nature and beauty, but at the same time were dedicated to their gods, who demanded that they sacrificed their enemies, as well as whomever might be available at other occasions. What more is known about the population of the capital in 1519?"

"Historians estimate that, although the actual population in 1519 is unknown, there were about 60,000 houses in all. Once the gardens and fields were in full production, as many as 350,000 inhabitants could have lived there." The more I saw of Tenochtitlan, the more impressed I was. "The Aztecs were an amazing people. I wonder how long that culture would have lasted without the invasion from Cortez?"

CHAPTER 20

TOGETHER

THE DAY AT Tenochtitlan was a busy one; by late afternoon I was ready to kick back with a cold Mexican beer and mull over the amazing things I had seen and learned. Johnathan said that he felt the same. So, we had Katrina take us back to the Holiday Inn, where we sat outside in the patio sipping a cold Mexican brew. Katrina said she had errands, but would return at whatever time we asked her to; we planned to eat again at the Mariposa, and we understood that Terri planned to meet us there.

After she left, I said, "Johnathan, what was the most interesting or fascinating thing that you saw today?"

"There was so much that it is hard to select one thing. I think that the overall complex of ruins, the size of the area and the layout of the city, was most appealing to me. Once you actually stepped into the compound and began to understand that you are part of a city that existed during the 14th and 15th century, it was amazing to me. What was your take-away?"

"Perhaps, more than anything else, once inside the city, I could actually visualize the Aztec way of life. Anyone with an imagination would be able to understand a day in that Aztec citadel. Looking at the steps of many of the ruins, you could even imagine blood running down from the sacrificial activities at the top. The codices that we saw were also impressive. Those documents and the murals helped to make the whole scene a reality. I came away believing that all of that was real, not just a scene in a play.

"I was extremely impressed with the National Museum, as well. I have visited the Smithsonian Institution in Washington, DC, and those museums are impressive, but maybe because one can walk among the ruins at Tenochtitlan, the Mexicans may have done an even better job of interpretation."

We spent another couple hours, along with a second beer, talking about the museum and the ruins, when suddenly we realized that time was getting away and we needed to get ready for dinner. Katrina was due in about an hour.

Katrina was right on time, and we piled into her car and were off to the Mariposa. We found ourselves in a traffic jam that seemed to move so slowly that I wondered if we would ever get to the restaurant. We eventually did, and Jerri was already there, sitting at our table from the previous night.

As she stood to greet us, I again realized what a beautiful woman she is. She was dressed to perfection to highlight her body and also to somehow reveal a personality that I had not detected earlier. She reached over and gave me a long hug and kissed me directly on my lips. I could not help but respond, and we stood together for several seconds before Katrina said, "Come on you two, let's order a drink. I'm ready for dinner."

While I was helping Jerri sit, the memory of Carol came washing over me. I knew then, more than anytime in the past, that I was in love with Carol. It was almost uncomfortable to continue with our pre-dinner drinks and the small talk that we shared around the table.

"How was your day," Jerri asked me.

"It was a truly remarkable day; Katrina was a great guide and interpreter. She seemed to know everything we asked about, and her explanations were all that I could have asked for."

After enjoying a small but tasty desert, Jerri seemed to zero in on me and asked, "Robert, what is your life like on St. Criox? I am surprised that you are still unattached. Do you have a girlfriend?"

"I do have someone special, although we have not made any future plans. I hope to do that soon however."

After a few minutes, I said, "Before coming to Mexico with Johnathan, I had gone to Miami to attend college, but things did not work out. I then joined Johnathan on this trip, and I have had an amazing time. I have seen ruins throughout the Yucatan and all the way to Mexico City."

I attempted to change the subject, but Jerri seemed intent on trying to find out more about me personally. If Carol had not dominated my thinking, I know that I could have steered Jerri to my bed, but that was not to be.

Although I enjoyed the dinner and the general conversation among the four of us, I was glad when Katrina said it was getting late and she needed to get some sleep. We agreed that she would pick us up in morning for another day. When asked where we would like to go, although Johnathan and I had not talked about it earlier, we decided that we would prefer to go back to the museum for our last day. Jerri left for home, and Katrina drove us back to the Holiday Inn.

When we arrived at the Holiday Inn, I went first to the front desk to retrieve a room key. The clerk said, "Sir, there is a letter for you. It arrived a short time ago." He handed me an envelope, and I immediately saw that it was from Carol. I think my heart must have jumped several beats; I could barely wait until getting into our room to read what she had to say. I must have physically leaped with joy or surprise because Johnathan looked at me like I was a crazy man.

"What did he give you?" he asked.

"It is a letter from Carol. I don't remember telling her we would be staying here for our last nights, but she must have figured it out."

I said, "Johnathan, I can only pray that her letter will address the deep feeling I have for her."

We walked into our room, where I immediately sat in a chair, opened her letter, and began to read. And what a marvelous letter it was! It was essentially a love letter! Not until reading it did I realize that I had missed so much of her feelings while we were together, but in her letter, she openly expressed them. To paraphrase, she told me that she did not realize how much she cared until she got back to Berkeley with her studies; she said that she was having difficulty getting back into her thesis because she could not concentrate.

Most of her letter explained that she did not know how I felt, and if I was as much in love with her as she with me, she had to know so she could go on with her life. If I loved her as much as she loved me, we should take whatever action necessary to be together.

In the next paragraph, she wrote, "I did not tell you much about my background. My father, when he died last year, left me with a sizable stipend to live on, and because of that I am able to meet you anywhere. We can find out if we truly are meant for each other. I so look forward to your response. I love you, Robert!"

I reread Carol's entire letter. Then I read it a third time. By the time I finished, I realized that Johnathan was looking at me very closely.

"Well, what's up?" he said.

Almost in a fog, I handed the letter to him. He took it and read it twice before saying, "Robert, that lady is in love with you; how do you feel about that? What are you going to do?"

"I've known for some time that I feel the same way for Carol, but I guess I did not have the confidence to tell her. But now I feel joyful and ready to tell her that I, too, want to be together. We need to see if we are really meant for one another or not."

"San Francisco time is behind Mexico City; you could make a phone call right now. But let me warn you, my friend, that any decision you make should be exactly about you, what is best for you in the long term."

I found Carol's number on a note in my wallet where I put it after she gave it to me. My hand was shaking as I dialed the front desk, which was necessary to make an international call. The front desk transferred my call, and I soon heard Carol's phone ring, far away on the western edge of the Continent.

"Hello," carol said.

"It is Robert, and I must first tell you that you are the love of my life. I think I have been waiting for your letter all my life. Carol, I love you very much, and I want us to be together always. How can we best make that possible?"

"Oh, Robert, I hoped and prayed that you would call."

"Carol, I have known that I love you for many weeks, but I have been afraid to let you know. Finally, with your letter, I can openly express my love. Believe me, I do love you, and I want us to be together. You mention that you are able to meet me anywhere. I have a suggestion."

"Robert, I am so very happy that you feel the same way. Tell me what you have in mind."

"I can leave Mexico City tomorrow, and although I have a return ticket to Miami, I could get that changed to San Francisco."

"I have another idea," she said. "I could fly to Miami to meet your flight. We could spend time in Miami and we could learn more about each other. You might even want me to meet your parents on St. Croix. What about that?"

"That is a wonderful idea. I long to take you in my arms and love you. I realize that you are the love of my life. Your suggestion is a good one."

I had a difficult time getting off the phone. Talking with Carol about our love and our future together dominated my thinking. It took us another hour or so before I told her about my flight to Miami, where we would meet. She ended our conversation with, "Robert, my love. I will meet you in Miami when you arrive. You are my true love. I so look forward to being with you. Good night, my love!"

In the morning, when Katrina arrived to take us to the museum, I explained my change of plans, although Johnathan had decided that he would spend another day at the museum. Katrina dropped me off at the airport, where I changed my flight to an earlier one to Miami. I then called Carol, explained the change, and she said that she would meet me.

We met in Miami and spent several days and nights together learning that our love was real. We flew to St. Croix to meet my parents, who seemed to be exceptionally pleased with Carol. A few days later, we flew to San Francisco, where we moved into Carol's apartment in Berkeley so that she could complete her thesis. I roamed the countryside until I found an apartment in Santa Rosa and a job at a travel agency. Soon after her graduation, we moved to Santa Rosa and began a life that we had only dreamed about.

It wasn't long before we began talking about marriage. Both of us had been raised in a Christian home. We planned to raise any children as Christians, as well. One evening after dinner, as we were sitting and talking about our adventures in Mexico, Carol made a suggestion that I immediately agreed with. "Let's get married and invite Johnathan and Katherine."

I looked at her a few minutes, and said, "I love your idea. I am more than ready to marry you, and It would provide us both the opportunity to see our friends again."

We immediately began to plan for the big event. Johnathan and Katherine were contacted, and both were excited and agreed to be part of our wedding. Johnathan agreed to be my best man, and Katherine said she would love to be Carol's bridesmaid.

Neither Carol's mother, or my parents were able to travel for medical reasons. My parents had already met Carol, and they were disappointed they were not able to attend the wedding.

Our wedding was extra special for several reasons. First and foremost, Carol and I were marrying our best friend, and our two closest friends were there to help us. It was a truly marvelous affair.

www.ingramcontent.com/pod-product-compliance
Lightning Source LLC
Chambersburg PA
CBHW021446070526
44577CB00002B/277